Member Tips and Projects

Member Tips and Projects

Handyman Club of America
Minneapolis, MN

MEMBER TIPS AND PROJECTS

EXECUTIVE DIRECTOR   Tom Sweeney
VICE PRESIDENT, PRODUCT MARKETING   Mike Vail
PRODUCT MARKETING DIRECTOR   Cal Franklin
BOOK PRODUCTS DEVELOPMENT MANAGER   Steve Perlstein

DESIGN AND PRODUCTION   David Farr, *ImageSmythe*
CONTENT EDITOR   Roy Barnhardt
COPY EDITOR   Jennifer Block
PHOTOGRAPHY   Scott Jacobson, Jerry Robb
SET CONSTRUCTION   Blake Stranz, Jim Shrack

COLOR SEPARATIONS   Clarinda Color
Printed and bound in the United States

ISBN 0–914697–72–2

Handyman Club of America
12301 Whitewater Drive
Minneapolis, MN 55343

foreword

Sharing home and shop tips and showing off special projects is as much a part of membership in the Handyman Club of America as is receiving the official Club magazine, *American How-To,* or testing tools through the Member Tested program. I know because of the tremendous response we get to the Tip Trader and Handy-Works sections that appear in each Club News. In fact, we receive so many great submissions each month we don't have room to publish them all in the magazine.

The tips we've collected in this volume can help the average handyman in many ways. Some will save you money. Others will save you time. But most of the tips will simply make difficult tasks a great deal easier. They come from professional tradespeople, gifted amateurs, and dogged trial-and-error experimentation—the kind of hard-earned lessons you will continue to find useful for years to come.

If you have been waiting patiently to see your tip published, you may find it here. You're also in luck if you are the type of member who likes to take a second look at a clever idea as you are about to tackle something similar, months or even years after the idea is published. This new member tips book contains dozens of hints and tips that have never appeared in *American How-To.* It also features many of the tips and all of the HandyWorks projects that have appeared since the magazine was launched in November 1993.

To compile the book, we selected the best tips members submitted. Then *American How-To's* Associate Editor Blake Stranz and club member Jim Shrack validated many of the concepts and prepared the props for the photos you see here.

Congratulations—and thanks—to all the members who made this book possible.

Tom Sweeney

Tom Sweeney
Executive Director
Handyman Club of America

contents

Member Tips
and Projects

member tips

Dowel-Slotting Jig

Here's an easy-to-make jig for ripping or slotting dowels. Cut a piece of lumber to 1x1x4½-in. dimensions. Mark the center on the end and bore a hole (equal to the size of the dowel that you want to slot or rip) through its full length, using a drill press. Draw a centerline at the edge of one side. Mark this line with a band saw blade, and clamp a fence across the band saw table against the side of the jig. Then make a 3-in. cut along the line and clamp the jig to the fence. To slot or rip the dowel, simply push the dowel through the hole in the jig past the band saw blade.

Edward Warner
Scottsdale, Arizona

◀ Center Hole Correction

No matter how careful a person is when it comes to laying out a hole for drilling in steel, sometimes the punch hole is not dead on the mark. To fine-tune the location, position the punch in the same hole, angle it toward the correct location, and tap lightly. This actually moves the punch hole to the correct position. Then stand up the punch, and rap sharply to make a heavy indentation that your drill bit can follow.

Joe Martin
Troy, Missouri

Handy Mower Basket ▶

I mounted a discarded wire basket on my lawn tractor so it can be lifted off easily. It has proven to be very useful.
I place my clippers, weed spray, and radio in it. Any debris that I come across as I mow also goes in the basket.

C.A. Hazelwood
Leitchfield, Kentucky

Fastening to Edge ▶ Grain of Plywood

We know that screws do not hold well in the end grain of plywood. You can greatly increase the amount of holding strength by inserting a ⅝- or ¾-in. diameter dowel in the plywood to accept the screw. Bore a hole through the plywood about ½-in. from the edge. Insert a glued dowel and bore a pilot hole before driving in the wood screw. Cut and sand the dowel so it is flush.

Chester Blank
St. James, New York

▲ Multi-grit Sanding Drum

On my 3-in. drum sander I placed half of a fine-grit sleeve, and half of a medium-grit sleeve. I can rough and finish-sand without pausing to change sleeves.

C.A. Hazelwood
Leitchfield, Kentucky

◀ Crack Hider

When installing paneling over drywall (the correct way to install paneling), color the drywall black at the paneling joints. If any joints open a bit due to shrinkage or warping (and they always seem to), they will be less noticeable than if the drywall was white. Use a wide marker or heavy carpenter's pencil. The same method works when panels are installed directly on studs.

Joe Martin
Troy, Missouri

Lending Tools

Many folks frown on lending their tools out. I do lend my tools, but only to people that I am sure know how to use them and take good care of them. I also have a surefire way of knowing who has them and when they were borrowed. I keep a chart on a clipboard by my shop phone. When the kids or friends want to borrow a tool, I record who has it and where it is before it leaves the shop.

Joe Martin
Troy, Missouri

Drill-powered Jack

A scissors-style car jack, a power screwdriver (or a variable speed electric drill), and a small steel rod enables me to raise and lower my lawn tractor or car. Insert a length of ¼-in. diameter steel rod into the jaw of your drill (A "T" brazed on the end of the rod suits the fitting on the jack). You can raise or lower with a pull of the drill trigger.

C.A. Hazelwood
Leitchfield, Kentucky

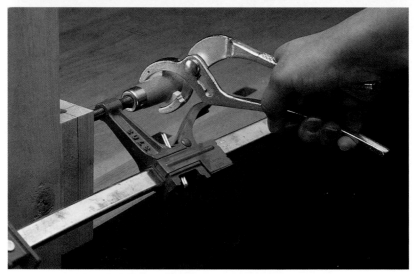

Easier Clamp Tightening

I have difficulty tightening bar clamps that have cylindrical wooden handles (such as the Jorgenson and Bessy). My hands slip on the smooth handles. My solution is to use a pair of connector pliers. These pliers, available at most electronic supply shops and some automotive supply stores, have rounded jaws with rubber inserts to keep from marring the anodized finish on twist-lock connectors. They are also a real help for those who don't have enough strength in their hands.

Kelly Kutz
St. Petersburg, Florida

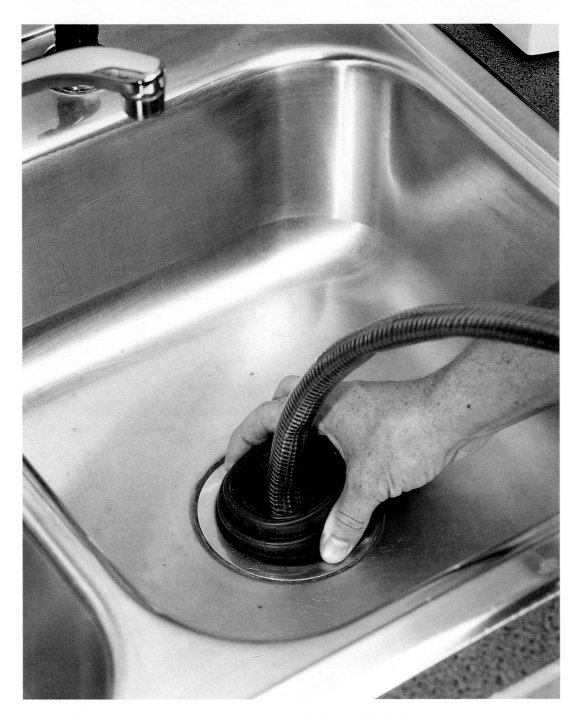

▲ Unplugging a Drain

Here's an idea that I've used for years ....
Now somebody has a patent on it—I still
think they saw me using my version! To
unplug a stopped drain, I cut a strip from
an old auto innertube and wrap it very
tightly around the end of a garden hose,
as many times as needed. It should taper
and fit snugly into the drain opening.
Then I just turn the water on to blast the
clog away.

Daniel Ostrander
Arkansas City, Kansas

Fishing for Wire

When pulling new wire to add switches
or receptacles in interior walls (or any
wall without insulation), I use a piece of
small chain as a fish. It is heavy enough
to fall down through the wall and not get
hung up. The electrical wire hooks on the
link quickly and is just as easy to remove.

Cliff Shaw
Westfield, Illinois

Stump Removal

Stump removal can be a daunting task. Even if you are able to cut the roots that extend to the side, the tap root can be nearly impossible to budge. I use my floor jack to lift tough stumps out of the ground. I set the jack on a board to keep it from sinking into the mud. Sometimes it helps to wet the ground around the stump before removal.

Carl Cooksey
Springfield, Virginia

Pipe Sander

To make a tool that can sand curved or irregular areas that are not accessible to a spindle sander, wrap paper around a length of PVC pipe and mark it for cutting. Apply two strips of ¾-in. double-sided tape lengthwise on the pipe. Place one edge of the sandpaper at the middle of one tape strip, and then roll it around the pipe to meet the starting edge. It's a good idea to have several pipe sanders, each with a different diameter.

Thomas Terstegge, Sr.
Terra Haute, Indiana

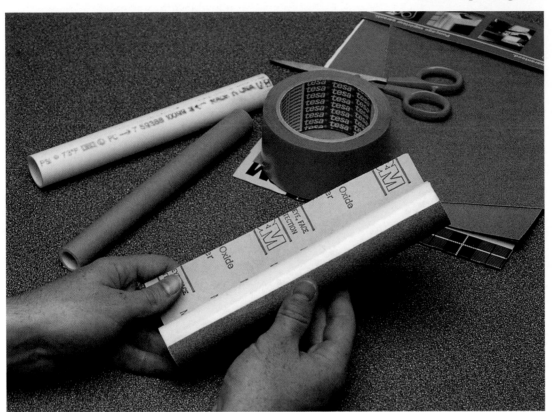

◄ Beveling Dowel Ends

Remember those old pencil sharpeners with the multi-sized dial? Need to bevel the ends of your dowel rods? Need I say more?

Mike Field
Fort Smith, Arkansas

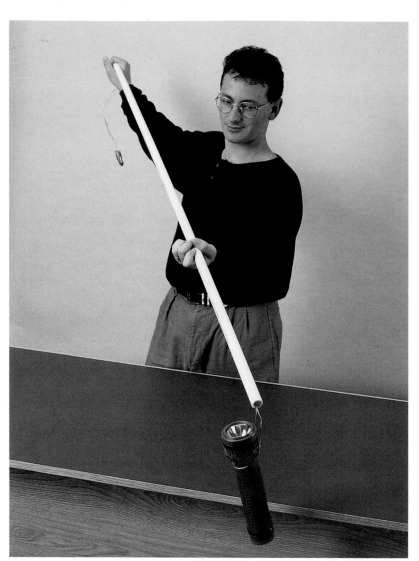

◀ Hard to Retrieve

While servicing a B-17 in the Air Force in the early forties, someone dropped a lighted flashlight into a gas tank and called me to help. I made a device with a length of plastic pipe and some wire to remove the flashlight, and have since used the idea many times to retrieve objects, large and small, that have been dropped out of reach.

Take any rigid tube that's long enough to reach the object to be retrieved, and a piece of wire or fishing cord that is more than twice the length of the tube. Tie the ends together and thread it down through the tube, leaving a loop big enough to go around the object to be retrieved. Put the loop over the object and pull the other end. Keeping the wire taut, lift the object out.

C.S. Masters
Opelika, Alabama

Acute Drywall Cornering Tool ▶

I do drywall finishing for a living. One day I was working in a room that had an acute angle at an inside corner that was impossible to tape and coat using my 6-in. knife. So I cut off the blade of an old 6-in. taping knife to match the corner angle, and it worked great!

Timothy Romig
Richfield, Pennsylvania

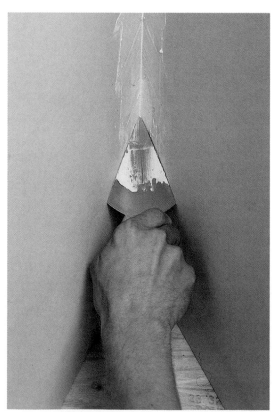

▲ Organized Sawdust

I collect fine sawdust from different woods and put them in film canisters, which I then label. As I complete a woodworking project that might need some fine finishing, I mix the sawdust with glue for filler. The color match is correct, the patch is easy to sand, and by storing the sawdust in the canisters it is easy to find.

Richard Mialki
N. Tonawanda, New York

Removing Glue

Have you ever gotten stuck on a glue-up that takes too long, and the glue starts to cure before you have a chance to clean it up with a damp cloth? Instead of water, try using denatured alcohol on your cloth. Don't flood the joint with the solvent, because it will migrate into the joint and break down your glue.

Kelly Kutz
St. Petersburg, Florida

▼ Router Bit Storage

I've always had a difficult time picturing the profiles made by various router bits, and I find it even more difficult to describe a profile to someone whose project I'm going to work on. I drilled holes in a 2x4 to hold my router bits; next to each bit location I routed the profile of the corresponding bit. I can see at a glance which bit I want, my bits stay organized, and I'm less likely to make a costly mistake.

Jennifer Clements
Anaheim, California

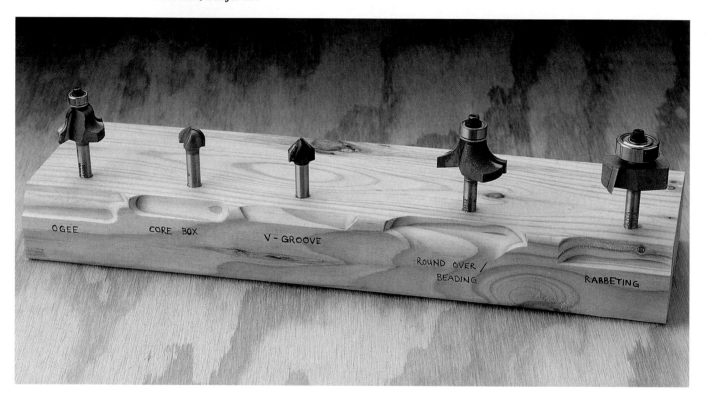

Easy Sanding Disk Installation

To quickly and accurately align the vacuum holes in pressure sensitive or hook-and-loop sanding discs with the corresponding holes in the tool pad, make a wooden holder with dowels, and stack a few discs facedown over the dowels. To install a new disc, simply place your sander over the dowels and onto the next disc.

Earl Mast
Etna Green, Indiana

Coloring Glue

When using wood glue on dark woods, or wood to be stained dark, tint the glue to make it less noticeable by adding a small amount of universal colorant (available at most paint stores). As long as the pigment is water-based and can be mixed without adding more than five percent water to the glue, it won't affect the performance.

Earl Mast
Etna Green, Indiana

◀ Easy Picture Hooks

One Saturday afternoon, while I was home watching our kids, I decided to hang a picture. I got everything ready and went to the garage to get my picture hanging hooks, but they were gone. I sat down to have a soda when, bingo—the soda can tab. What a perfect picture hanging hook.

Larry VanMaastricht
Waupaca, Wisconsin

Christmas Lights

My son and I devised a convenient and quick way of hanging outside Christmas lights on the house. We first measured the house in terms of 10-ft. lengths of white ¾-in. PVC pipe (the cheap stuff). I built a simple bolt-on jig for my table saw that kept one side of the PVC on the saw's blade. We then split the required number of PVC pipes lengthwise on the table saw so that a slot extended from one end of the pipe to the other, and threaded the wires into the pipe with the lights protruding. The pressure of the pipe keeps each light firmly in place and positioned at predetermined intervals. Two-to-three nails through pre-drilled holes is all that's required to hang each 10-ft. section.

I can hang a string of lights in a flash at the highest part of the gable; taking the lights down is a one person, 15-minute job; each section of lights folds up neatly, accordion-style, for easy storage in the attic until the next year. Our Christmas light strings seem to last longer because the majority of the electrical wire is protected by the PVC pipe and is not exposed to the sanding effect caused by winter winds against the rough edge of the house.

Martin McIntire
Redmond, Washington

◄ Repairing Chipped/ Cracked Porcelain

To repair chipped or cracked porcelain, Bakelite, or other hard-surfaced materials, use epoxy glue colored with oil-based paint. A well-stocked hobby supply store will have an almost infinite range of colors in small bottles.

Mix a small quantity of two-part epoxy glue (not the fast-setting kind). Add a drop of oil-based paint matching the color of the chipped or cracked article. Use only enough paint to color the epoxy since too much paint will affect the curing. Apply a dab or more of the mixture to the chipped or cracked area. Let it dry for 24 hours. Then lightly sand the dried glue until it is just level with the surface. Finish burnishing the area with rubbing compound followed by polishing compound to achieve a level and smooth surface.

D.W. Degen
Birmingham, Michigan

Drywall Helper

Hanging drywall on a ceiling can be a real hassle. To offset this problem, I made a stepped support that can be screwed to the joists and/or wall, as needed. It holds up one side of the drywall while I secure it.

Make the support with two 4-ft. lengths of a 1x6, fastening the pieces together with 1¼-in. screws, driven in from both sides. Bore 3-in. drywall screw pilot holes 16 inches on-center to match your joist/stud spacing.

To get the first sheet ready for hanging, screw the support to a side wall about ¾-in. below the ceiling joist. Then put the sheet of drywall over your head, and put one edge on top of the support. As you step up onto your scaffolding, push the drywall tightly against the wall, and slide it as necessary to get a tight fit on the end, securing the panel with screws.

Continue along one wall, moving the support as necessary. Then move the support over to a snapped chalk line, about 50-in. from the side of drywall just installed, and screw it to the joists. Repeat the procedure used for the first row, sliding the drywall into the support while you fasten it with screws.

Richard F. Jorgensen
Boise, Idaho

Custom Rubber Band Clamp

For odd-shaped or odd-sized clamping, cut an old bike or auto tire to the desired length and width (the wider the strip the stronger the clamp will be). Bond the ends together with rubber cement. For a good bond, overlap the pieces about 6-in., roughen the mating surfaces, and apply the rubber cement to both. Presto! A reusable, strong, rubber band clamp.

Earl Mast
Etna Green, Indiana

Accurate Cutouts in Drywall and Paneling

To mark the location of a plastic electrical outlet box in a wall so it properly fits drywall or paneling, cut off the flat head of two device screws (the ones that are used to hold a switch or receptacle in an outlet box). File down any sharp edges. Thread these screws into the outlet box, leaving approximately ¼-in. of the cut end sticking out. Similarly, cut another pair of screws and install them into a spare outlet box.

Secure the box in the desired location (see photo). Hold the panel in position against the box, and press firmly with your hand so the screws make indents on the back side (see photo) Remove the panel. Place the spare box on the panel so the screws fit into the indents. Trace the perimeter of the box onto the panel (see photo). Make the cutout with a drywall saw or utility knife, and you're ready to install the panel.

Robert F. Dollar
Oscoda, Michigan

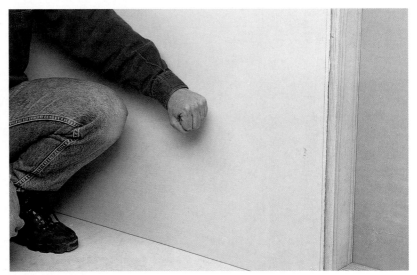

(Above, Left) Insert filed device screws into the outlet box, and position it in the desired location. (Above, Right) Position the drywall against the outlet box and press firmly, making sure the attached device screws make the needed indents. (Right) Align the box so the device screws fit the indentations. Trace around the box position, and make the cutout.

Removing Scuff Marks

To remove black marks from vinyl or linoleum, rub on a drop of 3-in-1 household oil with a clean rag.

Lorraine Meyer
Rochester, Minnesota

▲ Simple Measure

To quickly and accurately set my straightedge guide for cutting sheets of plywood with my circular saw, I cut a piece of ¾-in. plywood about 3-in. long, the distance between the edge of my circular saw blade and the edge of the base. I then mark the desired measurement on the wood, place the plywood piece on the mark, and position my straightedge guide against the other side of the plate. Note: You can't use the same guide for a blade that is thicker or thinner than the one used to make the guide, and you can't use it for another saw. If you have two saws, or might be using a thin-kerf blade, for example, make a second plywood piece and label it "B&D Thin-Kerf."

Kevin Pitzer
Galveston, Indiana

Wallpapering Time-Saver

Even though you're giving the room a fresh look with new wallpaper, you may want to maintain the screw and picture-hook positions. As soon as you remove the screw and picture-hooks, insert a 4d or 6d finishing nail into each hole as a temporary marker. When you wallpaper the area, remove the nails just before covering the holes, making sure to keep an eye on their positions. As the holes are covered, immediately re-insert the nails through the wallpaper, marking the positions.

Gary Schuman
Lockport, New York

Hook-and-Loop Sander Repair

When the hook-and-loop fastener on my sander became so worn that it would no longer hold the sanding discs, and the replacement pad was back-ordered, I had to do something. I went to the dry goods store and got a 2-ft. strip of 2-in. wide self-adhesive material. A little time spent with a pair of sharp scissors, and the sander was back in operation. It has been working great for over two years! Sure beats the $20 they wanted for a new pad!

Don Bledsoe
Adams, Tennessee

◀ Handy Paraffin Wax

Drill a hole in the end of a wooden hammer handle, and fill it with melted paraffin wax for a handy source of wax for screws and nails used in trim operations. Insert the points of screws or nails into the paraffin before driving them.

Ray Bartowiak
Westland, Michigan

▼ Dividing Materials Into Equal Parts

Here's a fast and foolproof method for dividing a piece of lumber (or other material) into equal pieces. For example, to divide a 5½-in.-wide board into three equal widths, hold a rule with the zero inch mark on one edge, and slant the rule until a number that can be divided by three is even with the other edge (in this example, 12). Then mark the board at the 4- and 8-in. marks. To divide the same board into four equal parts, look for a number that can be divided by four (for example, eight), and mark the board at the 2-, 4-,and 6-in. marks.

Ray Bartkowiak
Westland, Michigan

Coloring Concrete

Although standard advice says to mix all dry materials first, I found that I get a more even, consistent color throughout the cement if I dissolve the coloring in water and then add the water to the mix.

Robert Collins
Guntersville, Alabama

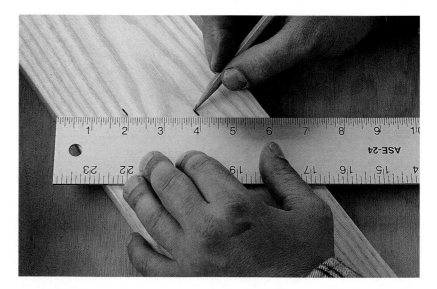

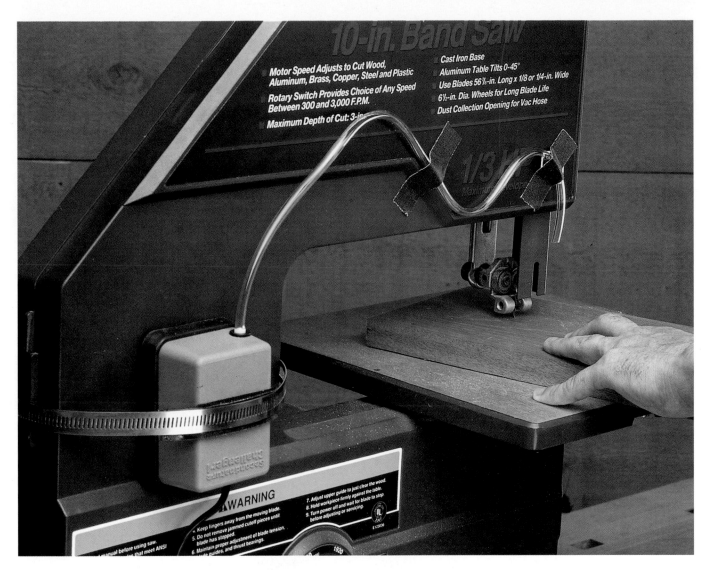

▲ Band Saw Blower

If your band saw blower is not working (or if your saw doesn't have one), you can use a fish tank air pump to blow your dust away. Mount it to your saw stand with a strap and run the air line hose up and onto the arm, strapping it so it is out of the way of your of lumber and blade. You can wire it to go on with the tool, or have a separate switch.

Carla Smith
Canton, Missouri

Paint Storage

For storing leftover paint of one quart or less, I take plastic bottles (from bleach or laundry detergent), wash them out and label them. I also put plumber's Teflon™ tape around the threads of the bottle for a better seal. That same trick is also good for tubes of glue or wood putty; the tubes are easy to open, and the materials remain like new.

Sam Alexander
Sun City, California

Knock-apart Bookcase

When I was in college, I needed a desktop bookcase that could be knocked down rapidly and just as easily reassembled. Even if such an item had been available, I would not have been able to afford it, so I had to make one. I had no machine tools available, so I had to do it all by hand. I used pine board, and when it was finished and varnished I wasn't ashamed to admit that I'd made it. The holes in the sides had to be a smooth and snug fit for the projections on the shelves, and the holes for the locking pins had to be correctly placed so the pins would fit tightly against the sides.

By removing the pins it was possible to take the bookcase apart for travel, and reassembly was just as easy and fast. All parts had identifying numbers hidden, when assembled, to make sure of a perfect fit. A half century later, after dozens of disassembles and lots of miles, it is still as solid as it was the day that I finished it.

John Braun
Lake City, Florida

Paint Can Tip ▶

The next time you finish up a paint job, draw a line on the can with a felt-tip pen to indicate the paint level before you seal it. After sealing the can, enter the date and the area where the paint was used. When it comes time for touch-up work or cleaning out the garage, you can see instantly how much paint is left in a can, how old it is, and where it was used last.

Robert Birkholz
Sun Lakes, Arizona

Flush–Cutting With Router

Flush-cutting router bits make trimming laminate easier and faster, but these bits heat up rapidly and may damage your project without the proper precautions. I apply a light coating of petroleum jelly on the face of the laminate surface where the pilot surface of the bit will run. This prevents the bit from heating up and also helps keep the bit free of glue buildup. The petroleum jelly is easily cleaned up with mineral spirits.

Clifford Jameson
Kearney, Nebraska

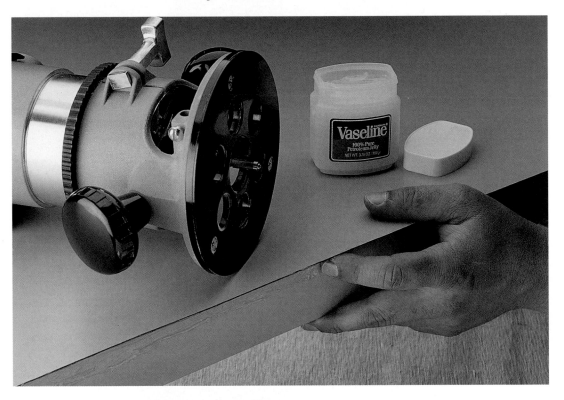

Shoe Polish Stain

During a recent trip to Africa, I watched native woodworkers finish wood with various colors of shoe polish. I make canes and walking sticks and, applying what I learned from these craftsmen, I now finish with paste shoe polish and power buffing. There's very little sanding, and very little mess—just a beautiful, rubbed furniture finish.

Harold Luvisch
Delray Beach, Florida

Weed Whacker Line Trick

If you have ever threaded a new line on your weed whacker and had a problem with the ends staying in the spool, try this simple fix. Thread the ends through the holes, take a match (or other heat source) and melt until a drop forms on the end. It won't pull through the hole in the spool, and you can wind the new line on, pulling it tight.

Donald Allen
Wheelersburg, Ohio

Molly Removal ▶

When you need to remove a Molly™ bolt from plaster or drywall, you cringe knowing it's going to make a large hole in the wall. To remove the anchor, take out the screw and insert the largest finishing nail that will fit in the hole. Hammer it into the anchor. This straightens out the crimped sides and let's you remove the Molly base, leaving only the original hole through which it was inserted.

Harold Baird
Decatur, Georgia

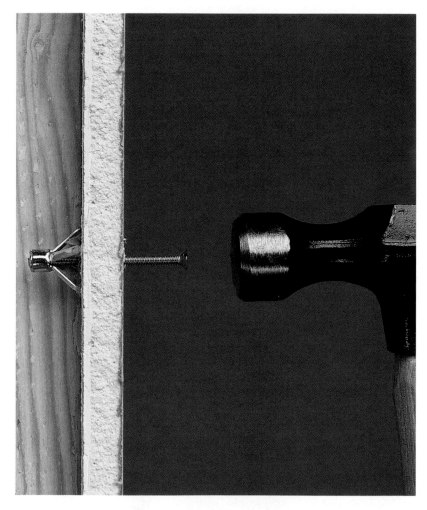

Greasy Hands

When you are using grease and find out you don't have any hand cleaner, just mix two parts petroleum jelly with one part corn meal.

Antoinnette Anderson
Maple Heights, Ohio

Edge-gluing Boards

Boards often bow and shift when you edge-glue them using bar clamps. To prevent this, I leave a ¾-in. gap between the boards and the bars. When the boards begin to bow, just insert some wedges between the bar clamps and the boards. The ¾-in. gap also allows you to wipe away the glue as it seeps from the joint, and prevents the bar clamps from marking the boards.

Tom Deveny
St, Louis Park, Minnesota

Siding Installation Helper

Here's a setup that will allow you to put up siding of any length (or width) by yourself. Cut a couple lengths of ¾-in. furring strips about 8-ft. long, and nail on evenly spaced lugs. The lug spacing should equal the desired reveal. Fasten each strip to the sheathing loosely with a 16d nail through a ¼-in. diameter pilot hole drilled in the top of each board. Position them so they are level with each other, and so the bottom lug is at the correct height for the first course. The siding is placed on the lugs and against the wall. After it is nailed, swing the strip out so you can set the next course in place, and so on.

John M. Farmer
Blackfoot, Idaho

Safely Routing Identical Small Pieces

I make ¾-in. thick doweled bases for small stand-up crafts, and some of the bases are as small as 2x3½-in. After cutting 50 to 100 of them, I rout the top edges with a piloted chamfer bit. Guiding such small pieces along my router table would put my fingers dangerously close to the bit, so I made jigs to suit each base from ¾-in. stock. Each base fits snugly in the jig, with one side extending ½-in. I can maintain downward pressure while guiding the base past the bit. It keeps my fingers well away from danger.

Robert Prentiss
St. Cloud, Minnesota

Tips on Setting a Toilet

I used to find it awkward to position a toilet over the mounting bolts without messing up the new wax ring. To solve the problem, I cut an ordinary drinking straw in half, and slide each piece of the straw over the mounting bolts. When setting the toilet in place, the added length helps align the bolts with the holes in the base of the toilet the first time, every time.

Diane Falk
Erie, Pennsylvania

Glass Cutting

When cutting glass, snap it immediately after scoring it. It tends to heal itself after a few moments and breaking it quickly will result in fewer bad cuts.

C.A. Hazelwood
Leitchfield, Kentucky

▲ Spin-Clean Paint Rollers

You need to spin a paint roller to get it really clean. Here's a simple spinner I made that fits in an electric drill. Straighten the metal handle rod of an old cage-type roller. Use a hack saw to cut off the rod just above the handle, and file off the sharp edges. File about ½-in. of the round end so that it has three flattened sides, and chuck it in the drill. Slip a paint-covered roller onto the cage and spin it inside a 5-gal. bucket of warm, soapy water. Then spin it for 30 seconds in a second empty bucket or garbage can. The roller will be clean and dry enough to use again immediately.

Gary Maurer
Ponca City, Oklahoma

Pulling Sign Posts

When I have to pull up sign posts, I use a
bumper jack. Place a 2x12-in. scrap of
wood on the ground at the edge of the
buried concrete, and set a bumper jack
on it next to the post. Wrap a tow rope or
a chain tightly around the post at ground
level, pull it taut, and loop it over the
hoist part of the jack. The rest is simple—
just jack it up and out of the ground.

Greg French
Cibolo, Texas

▼ Better Chuck Key Holder

Here's a tip for anyone who has a power drill that requires a chuck key. With this chuck key holder you'll never spend time looking for a misplaced chuck key, and its handle will give you added leverage for tightening.

Drill a hole in one end of a short dowel. For a tight fit, the diameter should be slightly less than that of the chuck key handle. In the other end, thread a screw eye with an eyelet large enough so that it will fit over your tool cord. Consider whether you want it to slide easily or clamp tight. Tap the handle of the chuck key into the wood rod. Pry open the screw eye, place your cord inside, and close the eyelet.

Edward Stanko
Niles, Illinois

A Good Wax Job

Periodically, I paste-wax my machinery tops to protect them. But for regular maintenance, I just rub the tops with a piece of wax paper that I keep in my apron pocket. It keeps the tops slick and rust free.

Joe Martin
Troy, Missouri

Wind Blown Plumb Bob

If the wind keeps blowing your plumb bob off the mark, and you don't have a 40-pounder on hand, make a fresh dot in the bottom of a jar, and fill it full of water. Lower the bob into the water, and line the dot up with your now-stationary plumb bob.

Eric Hanson
Berthoud, Colorado

A New Pattern Material

9x12-in. laminating plastic from an office supply store (about $20 for 50 sheets) works great for pattern making! Best of all, you can feed the plastic through ordinary copiers, so your patterns will be identical every time, and enlarging or reducing is a snap. I just peel off the backing and apply the plastic to the wood I am going to saw. This also prevents the chipping that you would normally get with scroll saw work, especially when cutting fragile material like ⅛-in. birch plywood. This pattern material is a lot easier to peel off than those applied with spray adhesive.

Jack Williams
St. Joseph, Illinois

▼ Plumb Bob Line Mess

Tired of trying to untangle a plumb bob line? Burn or drill a hole through the bottom center of a film canister, and insert the end of your plumb bob line through from the inside. Knot it off outside. You can stow up to 20 feet of dry line by winding it on three fingers and stuffing it in the canister. Tie the bob on that end, and let the "snap of the cap" keep the plumb bob and the line tangle-free.

Eric Hanson
Berthoud, Colorado

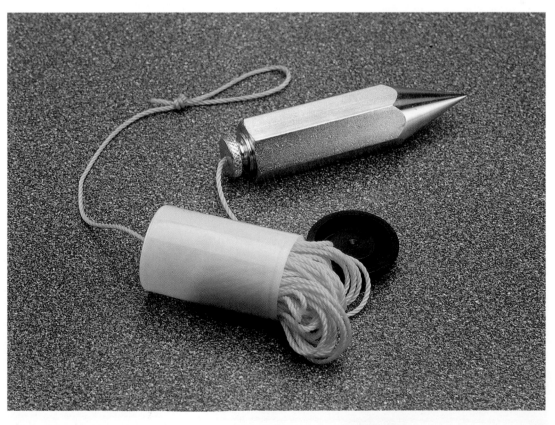

▼ For Very Messy Liquid Cleanups

If you have a particularly messy liquid cleanup for your Shop Vac™, and don't want to contaminate the can (or if you don't have a wet-dry vacuum), this setup lets you catch the liquid in any discarded drywall compound bucket or barrel that has a tight-fitting, removable top.

Drill two holes in the lid. Attach the hose from your vacuum to one hole, and a second unattached hose to the other. Turn on the vacuum, and the messy liquid will fill into the bucket without contaminating the Shop Vac chamber (or your regular vacuum). Watch the liquid level and dump it before it gets high enough for the vacuum to suck any in.

J.R. Riddle
Hamlin, Texas

Molding Storage

I recently salvaged several lengths of plastic rain gutter (10-ft. lengths). After tripping on them in the shop for a while, I decided I would have to use them or throw them out. Not wanting to do the latter, I used them to make horizontal shelving units to hold items such as molding, copper tubing, drywall corner bead, conduit, plastic pipe and any other lineal items that fit in the gutter.

Fasten the plastic gutter to a 1x4 with self-tapping sheet metal screws. Fasten the 1x4 to 4-in. shelf brackets that are attached to the wall. Presto! A 10-ft. container shelf for hard-to-store items. It works great.

Richard Brands
Taylorsville, North Carolina

Rope Inlays

Rope inlays in plain wood make an attractive frame. Inlay the material before mitering so the rope will be mitered at the same time as the wood. A contrasting rope color adds much to a plain frame. I color new rope by dipping it in stain and wiping off the excess with a cloth.

C.A. Hazelwood
Leitchfield, Kentucky

Better Pickup Bed

I have a small pickup truck, and as anybody who has one knows, you can't haul 4x8 sheets of plywood laid flat in the bed. Often they get pinched between the wheel wells, crushing the outside edges and converting your just-purchased premium-grade hardwood ply into shop-grade. To solve this problem, I made some short legs for two sawhorses, just long enough to hold the wood above the wheel wells. Remember, always use tiedowns to keep material from flying out of an open truck.

Kelly Kutz
St. Petersburg, Florida

▲ Emery Board Sander

When sanding small, recessed surfaces that are difficult to reach, such as grooves, use fingernail emery boards. They wear well, work quickly, and are easy to manage.

Val Buxton
Orem, Utah

Hanging Wall Covering in Hot, Dry Climates

In hot, dry climates, it is best to roll your pre-pasted paper in the water tray, according to the instructions on the label. However, it is also necessary to put watered-down glue on the wall. This gives it a double adhesive. Before we learned this trick, some of our wallpaper began falling off the wall as the weather got hot.

Dean and Sharon McClure
Artesia, New Mexico

Perforated Board Compass

Here's a fast and accurate way to swing an arc too large for a compass. Cut a 1-in. wide strip of perforated board (Pegboard) that's longer than the required radius (or make several lengths for future use). Position a pen or pencil so it fits snugly into a hole on one end. Secure the other end of the arm at the center point, and swing your arc. When you're done, hang this adjustable compass arm on the wall for your next project.

Jerry Ledford
Crowder, Oklahoma

▼ Dual Chalk Line

A Minnesota carpenter taught me this time saving trick. When using a chalk line to snap multiple lines, such as for roof shingles, it doesn't take long before the chalk becomes too faint to see. Then one person has to reel in to re-chalk, and the other person has to walk the length of the roof to retrieve his end of the line.

Instead, I keep two chalk reels in my vehicle with the lines tied together. That way, when the chalk wears thin, one person reels in and immediately exposes newly chalked line. When the chalk wears thin again, the other person reels in, and so on. Neither person has to do any walking. This method can save even more time than those fast-winding chalk reels.

Ray Ginsbury
Colchester, Vermont

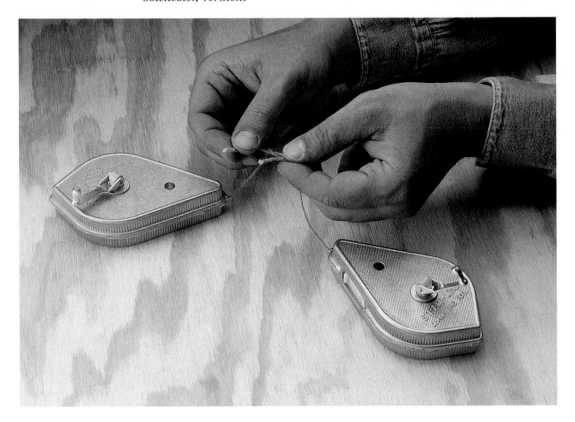

Keep the Dust Out

Shop switches and receptacle outlets are very vulnerable to dust. To keep the dust out, install foam outlet insulation covers under the cover plates. Also cover all unused receptacles with safety covers—the kind that are used to keep little children from sticking their fingers and other objects into receptacles. Just insert these plastic clips into the outlets and remove them when you want to use the outlet. Naturally, you get the safety advantage, too.

Tim Day
Dover, New Jersey

Hydraulic Holes

Digging holes for posts, plants, etc. in hard clay or dry sandy soil, especially when small rocks or large roots are present, can be done much faster and easier with the help of a small, powerful stream of water. An adapter (from garden hose to pipe thread), a pipe elbow, and a 4- or 5-ft. length of pipe are all that are required.

A ½-in. diameter or smaller pipe works best when large roots or small rocks are present, but it will have a greater tendency to splash the user. A larger pipe works better in sandy soil, and can be made more efficient by grinding the pipe to a sharp edge. This tool can be useful for transplanting shrubs or small trees. By using several short lengths of small-diameter pipe between the hose and the larger sharpened pipe, you can even dig a shallow well.

John Braun
Lake City, Florida

Loosening Soil

With only a ¼x5x36-in. piece of aluminum, a scrap of wood, and two bolts, many models of riding lawn mowers can be used to loosen rocky soil before grading. This method virtually eliminates hand raking and gets the job done in about one-tenth of the time.

You may need to drill a couple mounting holes in the front of the mower deck, and hacksaw notches in the top of the aluminum blade to clear linkage and supports located above the deck. I used scrap lumber to make a long wedge and mounted it between the deck and the blade to increase the angle of the blade.

For light soil loosening, the mower assembly is usually kept in the raised position. For very soft or rough conditions, however, I start with a high mower cutting-height position (the blades are never engaged, of course), then lower it as compacting and smoothness increase. The blade is secured with large wing nuts to ease installation and removal of the blade.

Thomas Rhodes
Warsaw, Virginia

Truly a Wonder

It seems that it's often impossible to get all the water out of a copper water line to make a repair. And if you don't, the dripping water prevents the pipe from getting hot enough for the solder to flow. Don't fret—roll a piece of soft white bread into a ball and stuff it into the end of the pipe. It acts like a sponge to hold the water back until you get the joint soldered. The bread dissolves and passes harmlessly through the valves. Be sure to remove any sink faucet aerators on the line, and avoid breads with seeds (they won't dissolve).

Dennis Orczykowski
Marengo, Illinois

Prevent Annoying Rolling

When I roll out wallpaper for gluing, it always tends to roll back up, especially when I get close to the end of a roll. My solution is to use plastic quilting clips. I slip a couple clips over the edge of the gluing board and onto the end of the wallpaper. They act like huge paper clips.

Richard Brands
Taylorsville, North Carolina

▲ Layout Large Radii

No room in a small shop to lay out a radius with a work piece flat? Hang a compass arm, such as a strip of perforated hardboard from the ceiling with the work piece standing on edge on the floor. Adjust the arm for desired radius and swing your arc.

Kip A. Smorey
Reading, Pennsylvania

Matching Patches

Wood plugs, spackling, and wood putty do not take the stain in the same way as the rest of the wood—I finally have solved this finishing problem. Here's my secret.

Save sawdust from the wood that you are working on in a small container. Put a small amount of satin polyurethane into a paper cup, then mix in sawdust a little at a time to make a smooth paste filler. After staining a piece of wood, press the filler into any crack or nail hole with a putty knife and tamp it down. The more you pack it, the better the finish will look. Be sure to leave the filler slightly above the wood surface. When the filler is thoroughly dry (overnight), sand the patch level with the rest of the board, and finish it to match the wood.

Joe Vanderlinden
Albany, New York

◄ Convenient Paint Refilling

To make filling the quart jar on my airless paint sprayer more convenient, I first pour the paint from either 1- or 5-gal. paint cans into clean, empty plastic milk jugs, using a large funnel. After the jugs are capped, they are easy to tote around on a job, and I can fill the sprayer bottle without having to deal with a messy funnel every time.

Robert Maass
Howell, Michigan

▼ Easy Center Finder

Here's how to make a handy center finder. Drill three evenly spaced holes in a length of 1x2 hardboard. The distance between the two outside holes should be greater than the width of the stock you want to center. Glue two short dowels in the outer holes. To use the jig, lay the center finder on the board and twist the center finder until the dowels touch the faces of the stock. Insert your pencil in the center hole, and slide the jig down the edge of the wood to mark its center.

Lois Luzier
Alliance, Ohio

Prevent Lime Buildup

I have never been satisfied with the commercial products that are meant to keep lime from building up in a humidifier (the water is especially hard in our area). So instead, each time I fill the humidifier, I fill the tank with cold water (as recommended). Then I dissolve a little less than ¼ cup of softener salt in about 10 ounces of hot water (to make it dissolve), and then add this to the tank. It does a much better job than the commercial products ever did.

Vaughn Werning
Fort Dodge, Iowa

tip trader

From the pages of *American How-To.*

tip trader

▲ Non–Slip Miters

When using a miter gauge on a table saw, the stock tends to creep toward the blade, resulting in an inaccurate cut. To prevent this, take a tip from C.R. Alexander of Topeka, Kansas: stick a piece of sandpaper to the face of your miter gauge. C.R. uses 80-grit emery cloth and adheres it with sanding-disc cement. You also could use an adhesive-backed abrasive sheet. To protect your saw table from scratches, position the paper or emery cloth high enough on the miter face so that it does not make contact with the table. To protect your stock, do not press it hard against the miter face when sliding it side-to-side to position the piece.

Do Not Disturb

If you need to remove a strip of earth from your yard for a sidewalk or pathway, take a tip from Life Member Jim Meek of Sublimity, Oregon. Instead of hand-digging the path's shape or excavating it with a Rototiller, rent a powered sod cutter. After laying out the path, set the sod cutter to a 2-in. depth. Most cutters only cut one foot wide, so make as many passes as necessary to obtain the desired width. When the path is cut, repeat the process. Now you'll have a perfect 4-in. trench with a uniform base of undisturbed soil for your walk. Undisturbed soil is the best base because it is least likely to settle.

▼ Custom Tote

Always looking for the right fastener in your shop or truck? Try this tip from Jeffrey Schweikart of Apache Junction, Arizona. Pick up a few Trophy (model 26000) three-compartment totes, (about $3 apiece at any hardware store.) While you're at it, buy a dozen plastic, new-construction electrical boxes for each tote. When you get home, take the nails out of the electrical boxes and nip off the nailing tabs with a pair of side cutters. Each tote will hold a dozen boxes; each box will hold about a pound of screws, nails or parts. And there's more: The totes stack on top of each other to save space, avoid spills and transport easily.

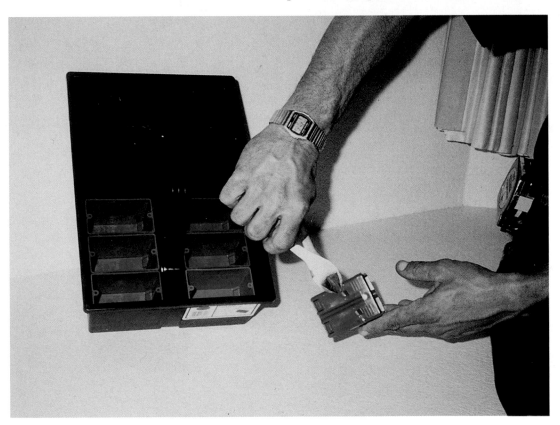

Paper Placer

Tired of struggling to line up the base of your sander with the dust collection holes on hook-and-loop or adhesive-backed sanding pads? Try this trick from Club member Robert O'Sullivan of Lake Katrine, New York. Take a small piece of scrap lumber and drill ⅜-in. diameter holes in it that correspond to the ones in your sander base. Then cut short pieces of dowel and install them in the holes with glue so they project about ⅜ inch above the surface. Round off the tops slightly for easy alignment. When you're ready to install a sanding disc on your tool, simply place it abrasive side down on the jig. Then set your sander over the dowels and press down. The sandpaper will be aligned perfectly every time so you will get the most out of your dust collection system.

Neat Idea ▶

Take some of the fuss out of cleaning paint brushes with this tip from Garvin Anfinson of Purdy, Missouri. Before starting a painting project, tightly wrap masking tape around the bristles at the ferrule. Garvin says it will keep errant bristles in line. He also says it will prevent the paint from seeping into the heel where it's hard to clean. Simply unwrap the tape before washing the brush.

Hold It!

With this tip from Club member Carl A. Kleppe of Milwaukee, Wisconsin, you can both support and wire a ceiling fixture while working alone. To suspend the fixture and provide room for working on the wiring, take a length of threaded rod that is the same diameter as the mounting rod that comes with the fixture (six to eight inches is a good length). Thread the rod into the receptacle mounting bar and hang the fixture from the rod. After the wires are connected, remove the rod and finish mounting the fixture using the shorter rod that came with it.

▲ Carburetor Cleaner

If you have a 2-cycle engine whose carburetor is gummed up
with old gasoline that has turned into varnish, don't try to
dissolve the deposits with starting fluid or carburetor cleaner,
warns John Strohmeyer. This Springboro, Pennsylvania,
member says they provide no lubrication for the engine on
initial start-up. Instead, after freeing the needle valve, spray
WD-40 into the carburetor. It will provide lubrication until the
gas-oil mixture reaches the cylinder.

Paper Punch

When Club member Don Schaufelberger of Columbus,
Nebraska, bought a new random orbit sander with dust
collection, he still had a large supply of perfectly good sanding
discs from his old sander that lacked dust extraction holes.
Instead of tossing them, Don made a simple punch by grinding
a sharp taper on one end of a short piece of ½-in. diameter steel
pipe. Now, after laying out a pattern of his sander's holes, he
simply stacks a couple of discs at a time on a scrap of soft wood
and punches the holes with a few taps of his hammer.

Up Tight

Club member Melvin Zimmerman of Ephrata, Pennsylvania, says the best way to loosen a threaded pipe that won't budge is to tighten it first. This should break the rust and allow you to loosen the pipe easily.

▼ Flatbar Functionality

Club member Larry Dyke of Montville, Ohio, found another use for a flat pry bar this past summer while building his new deck. By using a flatbar and a bar clamp, deck boards could be brought into alignment quickly and easily for screwing. The best thing about this system is that it doesn't require a joist like some other deck-aligning tools.

Globe Gripper

If you've ever had a hanging light fixture globe come loose from its base, it doesn't take long to figure out why. The set screws on the base have nothing to grip but the glass. This problem can be especially bad on ceiling fans that vibrate. To solve the problem, Chas Simpson of New Orleans, Louisiana, slipped a rubber band around the globe's rim. Now the screws have something to tension against, and they don't work loose.

▲ Finger-Saving Jig

If you sometimes need to rip small pieces of stock on your table saw, you'll appreciate this jig from Doug Arfsten of Sun City West, Arizona. It consists of a sled that rides on the rip fence with ¼-in. legs that push the stock. It also has an adjustable hold-down that keeps your fingers out of harm's way. When ripping very narrow stock, you can reverse the dowel so only the ½-in. diameter contacts the stock. If you want to make a jig like this, you need to dimension it to your own fence.

Pressed For Space

Need an easy-to-use, portable, adjustable work table? Try this tip from Club member David McCalmont of Bloomfield, New Jersey. Take an old ironing board and attach a scrap of plywood to it with carriage bolts. It's great for site work and cheap to build. Just remember, it's not designed to support the weight of benchtop power tools.

▲ Rat–Tail Filing

Club member John Kosut of Arlington, Virginia, uses a rat-tail file in his variable-speed drill to enlarge holes when he doesn't have the drill bit he needs. John says that by running the drill slowly in reverse, it is easier to prevent the teeth from bogging down in the material. It is harder to keep holes uniform and perfectly round when enlarging holes in thick materials, or when the size of the larger hole exceeds the diameter of the fattest part of the file. This technique works great in thinner materials, though, and with smaller-diameter holes.

Vac Snake

Instead of trying to push a fish tape through a long run of conduit, try this tip from Gregory Leafe of Sacramento, California. Tie a small scrap of cloth to a piece of nylon twine. Then working from the opposite end of the run, suck the cloth (and the end of the twine) through the conduit with your wet/dry vac. Some vacuums have a reducer to narrow the opening and increase the suction. With the twine through the conduit, attach your cable and pull it back through.

▲ Banquet Table

Here's a tip for members who use benchtop table saws to cut large stock. Sal Donato of Northvale, New Jersey, built this table to accommodate his benchtop saw. It consists of a 4x8 sheet of plywood and a dimensional lumber frame. By cutting relief slots for his saw to drop into, Sal has created a long extension for ripping, wide wings for crosscutting, and a left extension for cutting long stock to length, all of which are flush with the table top.

Keep It Under Your Hat

Do you have a hard time keeping track of the pad of paper you jotted your project measurements on? If so, you'll love this tip from Club member Larry Morgan of Concord, North Carolina. Stick a piece of 2-in. masking tape to the underside of a baseball cap's bill and write your measurements on that. Then when you need the numbers, lift your cap, take a look and replace your cap. You'll never waste time searching for a lost measurement again.

Seed Spout

James Cornell of Bedford, Pennsylvania, sends this back-saving tip. Instead of kneeling to plant seeds next spring, cut a piece of electrical conduit or ¾-in. PVC pipe about 40 inches long. Then place the pipe where you want the seed to go and drop the seed into place.

▼ The Hole Story

Here's another way to enlarge a hole that already has been bored with a hole saw. Take a hole saw that fits in the existing hole and install the larger diameter hole saw on the same mandrel. The smaller-diameter blade will serve as a guide for the larger one, keeping it centered on the original bore. Thanks to Club member Richard Pritchett of El Sobrante, California, for sharing this tip. He says it works great when he needs to enlarge a hole in a door for a new lockset.

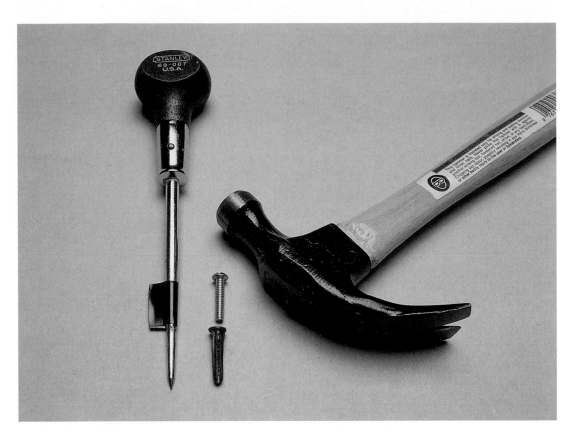

▲ Give It Your Awl

Club member Marshall Chun of Mililani, Hawaii, doesn't waste time drilling holes when installing plastic screw anchors. Instead, he wraps a piece of tape around a scratch awl to reflect the required diameter. Then he drives the awl into the drywall with a light tap. Marshall says his technique not only is faster, it's neater. There is virtually no drywall dust when you punch the hole with the tapered awl. The same can't be said for the traditional pre-drilling approach. The hole should be about 1/16 inch smaller than the thickest part of the screw anchor shank.

Coming Up Short

Here's a quick fix that Club member Ken Love of Colleyville, Texas, sent in. While replacing a toilet in a newly remodeled bathroom, the anchor bolts were too short for the base of the new stool. Since they were embedded in concrete, replacing the bolts would have been a pain. Ken's solution was to secure the stool with a couple of T-nuts. But before he did, he bent the T-nut prongs up so they wouldn't scratch the toilet. This also gave him something to grip when tightening the nuts. Be sure, however, to install the decorative cap retainer before you install the T-nut.

▼ Turning The Tables

Try this trick from Donald Newman of Edmore, Michigan, the next time you need to set your table saw's miter gauge to 90 degrees. Simply loosen the knob, flip the gauge over in its track and slide it against the rip fence guide bar. Since the blade is parallel to the fence and the fence is perpendicular to the bar, the miter gauge will be perpendicular too. Retighten the knob and flip the gauge back into position. The same technique works on router and bandsaw tables.

Wallpaper Saver

Hiding a hole in wallpaper made by a picture hanger, screw or hollow-wall fastener is always tougher than hiding a hole in a painted wall. But Perry Schrop of Akron, Ohio, plans ahead to avoid the extra work. Using a sharp utility knife, he cuts a small half circle in the wallpaper and folds it back out of the way. Then he bores the hole in the exposed wall. When it's time to conceal the hole, he simply fills it and glues the wallpaper flap back in its original position.

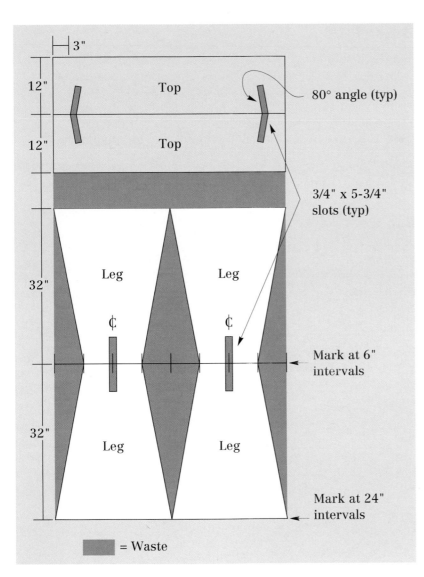

3"

12"

Top

80° angle (typ)

12"

Top

3/4" x 5-3/4" slots (typ)

Leg

Leg

32"

¢

¢

Mark at 6" intervals

32"

Leg

Leg

Mark at 24" intervals

= Waste

◀ Horse Sense

Douglas Barrett's dad taught him 20 years ago how to build a pair of saw-horses from a single 4x8-ft. sheet of ¾-in. thick plywood. Today, the Santa Maria, California, member still trucks a set around that lies flat in his pickup's bed. Start by cutting four strips from the panel across the 4-ft. side—two of them 12-in wide and two 32-in. wide. Next, take the 32-in. pieces and mark at six inch intervals on one 4-ft. side. Mark 24 inches on the opposite end. Cut as shown in the illustration so that you end up with four quadrangle legs that are 12 inches at the top and 24 inches at the bottom. Next, cut a ¾-in. wide x 5¾-in. deep slot in the top of each leg. Finally, saw similar-sized notches in the two 12-in. pieces, starting three inches from the ends and angled 80 degrees.

Drill Guide

When a drill press isn't available or convenient, how do you bore a series of perpendicular holes accurately with a portable electric drill? William S. Gnann of White Rock, South Carolina, uses a V-block he made from scrap to keep the drill bit perpendicular to the work, and a wood sleeve to control the depth of the bored holes. The guide block is simply two pieces of wood about two inches long, butt-jointed and glued together. However, it's important to make the guide block as square as possible to ensure accurate results. When using the guide, be sure the bit is in the corner and that the bottom of the guide is pressed against the work. The deeper the hole you're drilling, the longer the drill bit will need to be.

Sucking Up

Digging post holes in dry, loose sand with a conventional post hole digger can be a slow, tedious process because the sand tends to fall out of the jaws. But Richard J. Bukowski of Lake Orion, Michigan, gets the job done much faster by using his shop vacuum. He says that in loose sand, you can excavate a hole as deep as you can reach without any manual lifting.

Tray Liner

Painting contractor Dan Nuhfer of Warren, Pennsylvania, writes that his tried-and-true method for keeping roller trays clean is certain to help other Club members keep their trays spotless. Simply cover the inside of a clean tray with a plastic trash bag, pressing it into the corners. Fold the edges of the bag over the outside of the tray and secure them with masking tape. When you're done painting, pour the unused paint into a can, peel off the bag and dispose of it in a safe place. You can also use the bag to remove the roller cover.

▲ Sticky Situation

If you are tired of debris sticking to the sides of your duct tape rolls, you'll appreciate this tip from Scott Webster of Aiken, South Carolina. Sprinkle talcum powder on both sides of the roll after you buy it to eliminate the tacky edges. The edges won't stick to your fingers when you are using the roll, and nothing will stick to the edges when the roll is bouncing around in your toolbox or behind the seat in your truck.

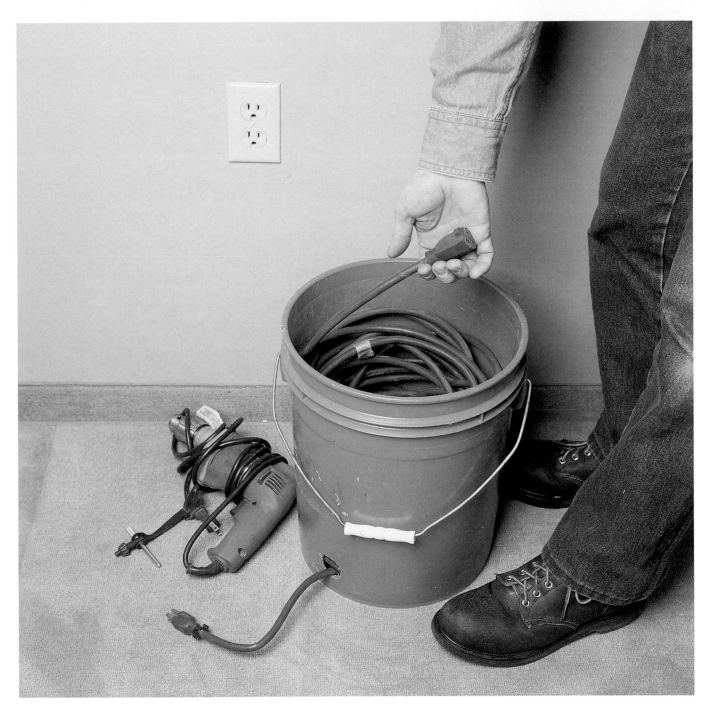

A Drop In The Bucket

For member Samuel Shaw of Ozark, Alabama, the time spent coiling his long extension cord after a how-to project is a mere drop in the bucket. Sam cut a hole in the side of a joint compound bucket just large enough to accept the male end of his cord. Then he fed the free end into the bucket to form a loose coil. When he needs to extend the cord, the last section in is the first section out, so there are no tangles. Sam admits the bucket takes up more space than the cord alone, but there's a silver lining. Even with a 50-ft. cord coiled inside, there's still room for Sam's electric drill or circular saw.

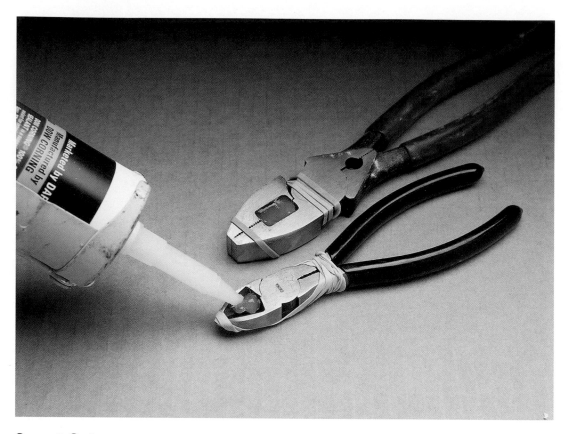

Smart Snips

You won't find diagonal cutters or lineman's pliers like Billy
Van Brown's in stores or catalogs. But you will want some in
your own toolbox before your next electrical project. It seems
the retired Fairfax, South Carolina, design engineer was tired
of tiny pieces of wire and insulation flying everywhere when he
trimmed the ends of wires while working on circuit boards and
other wiring projects. "I was always looking for those little
pieces, wondering whether they were hiding somewhere in the
circuit board where they could cause a short later on," he said.
Billy solved the problem by filling the pliers' cutter cavity with
silicone rubber. To improve your own cutters, first clean the
cavity thoroughly to remove any grease. Secure the pliers in
the closed position with a rubber band, and fill the cavity with
clear silicone. Let the silicone cure for a few days. Then slice
the silicone in half with a sharp utility knife. The next time you
snip a piece of wire, the silicone will hold the debris until you
release it.

Drilling Nails ▶

What handyman hasn't chucked a headless finish nail in a drill when he didn't have a thin enough bit to make a pilot hole? But member Bud Reckling of Rochester Hills, Michigan, puts a better spin on the practice. He first flattens the end of the nail into a chisel point with his hammer (shown here). The spade shape bores through hardwoods much faster and cooler than the round nail shaft.

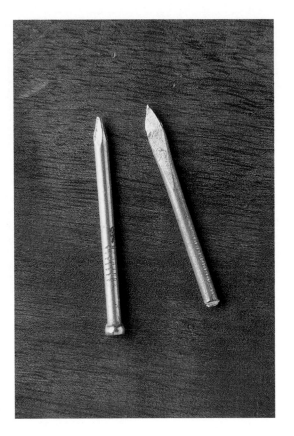

Not Just For Showers

Club member Joe Atler of Lodi, California, has found some unique uses for shower caps. He says he uses them as bucket covers to keep paint and other liquids from splashing out. They work well as emergency lids for tool buckets in the event of rain. He also suggests that you can cover your shoes with them so you don't track mud on carpeting. Best of all, disposable shower caps are inexpensive.

Less Mess

Sanding drywall seams and patches is a messy job, but Kenneth Muetzel of Pittsburgh, Pennsylvania, has found that he can keep the dust down by using a damp 3M O-Cel-O Sponge Scrubber (a cellulose sponge bonded to a synthetic fiber scrubbing pad). He uses the scouring side to sand and the sponge side to remove any remaining dust before he paints.

Bright Idea

According to Club member Harold Phillips of Lancaster, Ohio, a good way to keep light bulbs and sockets working well is to first turn off the circuit at the breaker box, then gently bend up the metal contact in the base of the socket. This ensures a good connection between the bulb and socket and prevents arcing.

Handycap Hammer ▶

Club member Dan McManus of Oswego, New York, works in the maintenance department at his local hospital. Since he fixes everything from rooftop air handlers to wobbly chairs, he's a big fan of tools that serve more than one purpose and limit his load. Instead of carrying a rubber mallet in his toolbox, Dan merely slips an old rubber crutch tip over his nail hammer (shown here) when he needs a no-mar blow.

Dust Fan?

Here is an inexpensive yet effective way to keep your shop relatively free of fine dust that escapes your primary dust- and chip-collection system. Take a window fan (the square box kind), and buy two furnace filters that are roughly the same size as the fan. Using duct tape, attach the filters to the fan grills on both the intake and exhaust sides. Turn on the fan, and it will filter dust from the air as you work in your shop. Thanks to Irvin Aaron of Birmingham, Alabama, for this tip.

Clean Your Nails

When doing woodworking and trim carpentry, especially on unfinished wood, oily nails can easily stain the surface. To prevent the oil from getting on your hands or on the workpiece, try this tip from Joseph Lenard of Wausau, Wisconsin. Put a little sawdust into your nail apron along with the nails. The wood particles will absorb the oil. Both your hands and your stock will stay much cleaner.

handyworks

handyworks

Asleep at the Wheel

When Steve Misturini of Lindenhurst, New York, decided to buy a race car-style bed for his son, Anthony, he was disappointed with store models. He thought the materials and workmanship were poor, and the mattress was nothing but a thin foam pad. He knew he could do better, so he decided to build a bed himself. The long-time sports car buff and former Corvette owner modeled the bed after a 1987 Corvette. It holds a standard twin-size inner spring mattress. The frame is pine and the body is birch plywood. The hood opens for storage. When Steve painted the piece, he included authentic-looking Corvette details such as racing stripes, headlights, and mag wheels. When Anthony's ready for bed, he swings open the door and hops in, ready to cruise through dreamland.

Look Before You Lift

Lack of masonry experience didn't stop Club member Rollin Joy from building this floor-to-ceiling stone fireplace facade. He hauled six to eight stones at a time to his Bellingham, Washington, home from a mountain road construction site where he was clearing timber. It took over a year to gather enough stones to complete the project. Now the voice of experience, Rollin offers this advice to fellow members who might be inclined to follow a similar path: Before you mortar the rocks in place, fit them together on the floor to get the best look, and mark the pieces. Otherwise, it's like putting together a giant vertical jigsaw puzzle by trial and error, with very heavy pieces and no plan to guide you.

Playmansion

Club member Bob Molloy of McMinnville, Tennessee, says he bent a few construction rules when he built this playhouse for his granddaughters. "You can throw away your square for this project," he says, "because everything is either curved or angled." Figuring out how to build this unique design took some careful planning. The curved rafters are cut from tight-grained 2x10 stock, and the door and window tops are arched to match the curve of the roof. Bob even cut the curved glass and turned the posts. He also made the house safe for his grandkids by installing GFCI-protected outlets.

▲ Big Desk, Little Desk

Hill Kulick of Miami, Florida, always wanted a rolltop desk, but he never seemed to find the time to make one. In the midst of building furniture for a custom doll house, Hill was inspired to build a miniature version of a rolltop that was featured on a magazine cover. He figured it would be a great way to see how it might function before he invested time and money building the full-size desk. The 6-in. model has working drawers and a tambour door.

Hill didn't like the layout of the slots behind the door, so he made some revisions to the design when he built the full-size red oak version shown here. He spent nearly a year, working an hour or two a day, making the real thing. Now that it's finished, Hill's life-size rolltop dolls up his living room.

A Garage and a Playhouse ▶

Club member Joseph Homrich of Defiance, Ohio, needed a place to store his lawn tractor. He couldn't find a ready-made shed that was appropriate for his scenic location, so he decided to design one himself. His first plan was for a 12x12-ft. structure that included an 8-ft. garage door. He figured his grandkids could also make great use of the space, so he decided to build a matching structure that would be used as a playhouse. Joe's skills as a pattern maker were useful in designing the project. When he needed to determine the proper roof pitch, he built a scale model. The buildings are slab on grade, with stick-framed walls and rafters. They are connected by a central breezeway. People often ask what the buildings are used for. Joe just smiles and tells them they are his garden houses.

In Good With His Mother-in-Law

Years ago, while working as a sawyer at a small mill, Club member Weldon Schwartz of Crystal, Minnesota, struck a deal with a customer. In exchange for cutting a truckload of wood, Weldon received a few choice cuts for himself, including a large slab of 110-year-old black walnut. Recently, he used the last of that wood to create this jewelry armoire. Weldon's design was, as he puts it, "shared at times with the wood's own desires." It features hard maple doors, which provide a striking contrast against the dark walnut. The only hardware are the magnetic door catches—even the knife hinges are made from wood. The final touch was a hand-rubbed tung oil finish. He gave the box to his mother-in-law for Christmas. She's delighted with it and figures it was worth the wait.

It Looks Better Than Concrete

Member Jim Buttner of Prior Lake, Minnesota, has a classic
split-entry home, with concrete block half-walls in the
basement. He's a professional cabinet maker, so when he
decided to finish his basement, he designed and built this oak
wall unit to cover the protruding half-walls. The top half of the
unit is entirely usable while the bottom portion is merely a
facade to cover the protruding block wall. Jim wanted the lower
cabinets to give the appearance of storage, so he added raised-
panel "doors" to complete the illusion.

Staying after hours at the cabinet shop where he works,
Jim built the unit in sections, then transported them home.
There, he assembled everything in place and affixed the unit to
the existing walls. Jim also installed the fireplace and hearth
and built a wet bar. The entire project took nearly two years.

Determined Woodworker

Robert Myron loves woodworking. When this
North Branford, Connecticut, member developed
multiple sclerosis a number of years ago, he was
determined that the disease would not stop him
from pursuing his hobby. He started by making
his workshop accessible, building benches that
enable him to work comfortably from his
wheelchair. Over the years, he has outfitted it
with high-quality woodworking tools. Robert
modifies plans so he can do projects unassisted.
By cutting stock into shorter lengths and
keeping project components small, he can place
pieces across his lap and wheel them from one
bench to another. For example, this video hutch
was built in two parts—an upper and lower
section. Made from black walnut, the cabinet
took Robert 123 hours to build and finish.
When people express their surprise at his
accomplishments, Robert shares the philosophy
that he lives by these days: "I like to think of
what I can do instead of what I can't do."

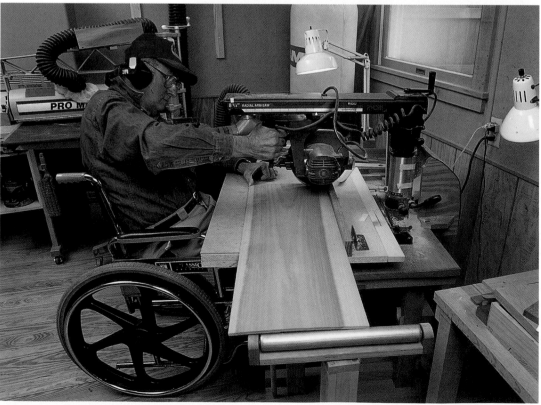

Gracious Gazebo

Newport Beach, California, is lucky to have Ron Feldhaus. A handyman for more than 30 years, this Club member does everything from minor plumbing to complicated carpentry. He built this cedar gazebo last spring for a friend who needed it completed fast for his daughter's college graduation party. Because time was short, Ron started with a kit and recruited three helpers to speed assembly. Despite its open air charm, the structure is built to stand up to the elements. The cedar shake roof is preserved with ultraviolet-blocking stain and the rest is finished with marine paint. Removable screens and a large paddle fan keep it as comfortable within as it is beautiful without.

Scrappy Fence

How do you build a long privacy fence with mostly short boards and a budget of less than $2 per running foot? To solve this problem, just ask retired school teacher Don Warner of Lawton, Oklahoma. The Club member bought 3,000 scrap pieces of treated pine from a local factory for $400. He made the patchwork modules you see here using only a table-mounted circular saw and a hammer. It took him four months to complete the 210-ft.-long structure. He deserves extra credit for this assignment.

A New, Old-Looking Bar

Club member Randy Horton and his wife, Margaret, built this old-fashioned bar from the ground up. Their 100-year-old Swartz Creek, Michigan, farmhouse sat on a shallow cobblestone foundation over a dirt-floor cellar. So they jacked up the house, tore out the old foundation and replaced it with a proper one. The couple designed the project on their computer and finished the walk-out basement themselves. They used mahogany beadboard paneling around the bar and custom-framed the mirrors. Randy even trimmed out the tops and the bottoms of the classic fluted columns with his router.

It Sure Looks Expensive

John Schuler teamed up with his daughter, Jeanine, to build this storage unit for her master bedroom. Jeanine sketched out the concept, and John figured out all the dimensions. By combining particleboard, pine, plywood, and decorative molding, the Olympia, Washington, Club member managed to

keep the materials bill just under $350. He completed the project in just six weeks. While the recessed panel doors and Colonial hardware look traditional, the cabinets are full of clever surprises. The drawers on the right side actually are drop-front doors that open up to shelves. And hidden behind one of the lower square doors is a roll-out laundry basket.

The retired lithographer spent a career achieving art and order in two-dimensional objects. It looks like these three-dimensional projects are half again as good.

▼ A Golden Hutch

Fewer trees dot his yard, but Harry Kern says that's a small price to pay for his golden anniversary gift to his wife, Ann. The Wellston, Michigan, Club member built this corner hutch from red oak trees he cut down in his yard. After drying the rough lumber for three months in his shop, Harry planed and shaped the wood with a 10-in. planer and a table saw, and routed it out for the glass panes and cupboards. He finished the piece with an oil stain and spray-applied clear lacquer.

Harry has been working wood since he was about 14 years old. One of his favorite pastimes is making wooden clocks. Two of his creations are pictured here on the hutch. Ten more pass the time in his workshop. Fortunately, Harry has all the time he needs to pursue his woodworking projects. We should all be so lucky!

▲ Priceless Secretary

Since retiring from his bank job in 1980, Club member Ken Mayhew of Pembroke, New Hampshire, hasn't slowed down a bit. He spends most mornings in his workshop building pine furniture, including curios, hutches, tables, bookcases, and toy boxes.

One day Ken decided to break from his routine. Fifty hours later, this cherry secretary desk and chair were finished. The desk features tapered legs, a dovetailed top, walnut and maple inlays, and hand-carved fans. Ken says the local antique shop offered him $1,400 for the desk, but he turned them down. It's hard to find a good secretary these days.

Stylish Shed

Maylene, Alabama, member Larry Johnston and his wife, Stephanie, wanted a shed to store their garden tools and match the style and look of their home. So after a trip to the local home center, the couple launched their first building project. Using a how-to book as their only guide, they built this hip-roofed structure, complete with a cupola for ventilation. The 10x10-ft. shed is constructed on a wooden platform supported by concrete footings. They used short posts at the back because the land was sloped. All it needs now is a small ramp at the doors.

Larry says the hardest part of the project was framing the roof. They could have run power to the shed but they chose not to. The coach lights, they shared, are just for show.

Drywall Self-Help

Club member Tony Bitts of Lynnwood, Washington, is into self-sufficiency. The general contractor has built six houses, including the one he now lives in. He designed the lift you see here so he could install drywall on ceilings without a helper. He made the device from scrap 2x4s he had left over from a job. The two ends are assembled with nuts and bolts. He used heavy-duty swivel casters on the four corners so he could wheel it around. To use the apparatus, Tony places a sheet of wallboard on the top and raises the inner frame until the panel touches the joists. Then he secures the brackets in the extended position by inserting 16d nails into pre-drilled holes in the center vertical piece. Tony says the hardware makes it easy to assemble and disassemble the contraption when he needs to move it from room to room or site to site.

Of course, Tony could have bought or rented a commercial drywall hoist, but that wouldn't have done much to satisfy his inventive spirit. Like many of us, Tony is a diehard do-it-yourselfer.

Faster Than a Horse

Member Joe Golden of Wolcott, Connecticut, knows how to improve on a good thing. This full-time antique restorer and spare-time woodworker has built a good deal of furniture and quite a few traditional rocking horses. When his son, Joey, requested a rocking motorcycle for his third birthday, Joe started with purchased plans and then added a little spin of his own. First, instead of using plywood for the body (as suggested by the plan) he used solid ash milled from a neighbor's felled tree. Then he added a couple of other embellishments, such as a headlight and taillight. The spindle, grips, and lights were all turned on Joe's lathe. While Joe doesn't count motorcycling among his hobbies, his in-laws are long-time enthusiasts. With a wonderful motorcycle like this to start with, Joey may graduate to the real thing some day.

Congratulatory Armoire

Steve Boyd of Sparta, Tennessee, designed and built this armoire for a friend who was looking for the perfect wedding gift for his daughter. A page from a catalog was Steve's sole inspiration.

His design includes a VCR shelf, a sliding swivel TV shelf, pocket doors on the top half of the piece, and a storage shelf behind the bottom doors. He used 120 bd. ft.of cherry cut from trees on his own property. The finished cabinet stands 6 feet tall and took about 50 hours to complete. Both Steve and the recipient are pleased with the results. The armoire is not the first project Steve has tackled. A full-time carpenter for the past two years and part-time craftsman for 15 years before that, he has built his own log home as well as various furnishings such as china cabinets and bookcases.

▲ High-Rise Deck

How do you add a 2½-car garage and at the same time nearly double your usable yard space? Club member John SerShen of Chicago, Illinois, replaced his dilapidated garage with a new, larger one and added a 720 square foot deck in the process. Except for laying the block walls, John built the entire structure himself. First he muscled the lumber from the ground to the top of the walls. Then he rolled the joists into position, secured them, and laid the deck. He didn't mind the solo work but he has vowed to work more safely in the future. While carrying sheet goods on the roof, a strong gust of wind pushed him and his load right off. Even though he suffered a broken leg in the fall, John still managed to finish the project in just over four months.

◄ Beautiful Buffet

Otis Dahl isn't one to let his talents—or underutilized living space go to waste. A retired salesman who has been a woodworker for about 11 years and a remodeler even longer, the Bella Vista, Arkansas, member has built a hutch, curio cabinets, tables, and other pieces to provide attractive storage for his family's valuables. Otis built this solid oak buffet from his own design. Dishes are stored behind the two side doors, while drawers in the top and bottom hold silverware and linens. The center section protrudes 2 inches beyond the sides, and the resulting angles give the buffet even greater visual appeal. The piece was assembled with biscuit joints and finished with a light oak stain and polyurethane finish.

Something Fishy

Retirement hasn't slowed down Timothy Perron of Tunkhannock, Pennsylvania. Over the last 1½ years, when he wasn't working on restoring his 135-year-old home, Timothy built this Oriental-style fishpond with a raised garden and waterfall. The pond is home to both koi and fancy goldfish.

All of the work was done by hand, including excavating the soil, pouring concrete, and hauling stone from a wooded section of his property. Water is supplied to the falls and circulated in the pond via a submersible pump. For evening drama, Timothy installed low-voltage lighting around the pond, all hidden from view. Construction of a garden teahouse at the water's edge is nearly completed. Now that winter is here, Timothy is using his spare time to build a dining room set—and, no doubt, to hatch new ideas for future projects.

A Real Treehouse

When a windstorm damaged the top of their pin oak tree, Don
and Trudy Post saw opportunity rather than disaster. Their son,
Colin, was about to celebrate his ninth birthday and the tree
would be the centerpiece of the perfect gift. Working together,
this family from Fairfax, Iowa, built a treehouse for Colin, using
the tree's trunk as the central base. The structure features a
treated deck, a cargo net, a rope ladder, tire swings, and a full
swingset. The project provided a perfect setting for giving Colin
some basic lessons in construction. Starting with a scale model,
Don and Trudy explained each step of the building process.
Then together the family swung their hammers. The Posts
figure the lessons and the treehouse should last a lifetime.

An Award–Winning Award Case

The people at the United Technologies plant where Gilroy, California, Club member Mike Hughes works have long been aware that he's an avid woodworker. So when the company needed a display case for the lobby, the human resources director asked Mike to design and make one. The 7x12-ft. oak and glass case is nearly as big as Mike's shop, so he built it on his patio under a temporary tarpaulin enclosure. He then transported the three 4-ft.-wide sections and the base frame to the office, where he reassembled them and attached the face. Mike's now working on a storage cabinet for the company's photography department.

Never–Ending Project ▶

This project started simply enough. Jack Saylor's friend asked him to build in-wall cabinets for his TV and other electronic equipment. But the back sides of the component boxes looked odd where they protruded into a guest room, so the friend asked the Napa, California, handyman to incorporate them into the desk and shelves shown here, turning the guest room into an office. Then came the idea to add storage cabinets and drawers beneath the window. Sound familiar? We've all worked on projects that mushroomed like that, right?

▲ Chilly Dog

It's no wonder Snapper is looking pretty darned smug. His owner, Club member Michael Brown of Boynton Beach, Florida, built him an air-conditioned doghouse. Mike modified the chiller system from an old soda dispenser to create the refrigeration unit. A concealed blower in the doorway creates an air curtain that keeps the cold air in and the bugs out. He says it costs less than $6 per month to operate. Michael built the doghouse itself with materials left over from other projects.

Entertaining Entertainment Center

Every room in Jim Talberg's Centerville, Minnesota, house has
at least one item that the handyman/construction supervisor
built, but this entertainment center is the biggest. The upper
doors slide away to reveal the TV, VCR, and reel-to-reel tape.
Behind the lower doors are roll-out shelves for the turntable,
cassette player, and tape storage. Jim wanted the look of an
old-fashioned cabinet like one his grandparents had, so he used
standard pine and left most of the edges square. The biggest
challenge, says Jim, was getting the swing-out hinges, designed
for 3/4-in. wood, to work with the thicker rails on his doors. By
experimenting with rail thickness and cutting a deep mortise
for the hinges, he eventually got the doors to swing out to the
point where they could slide into the cabinet.

Putting Down Roots

As an Air Force officer, Cliff Miller moved too frequently (22 times in 35 years) to even bother setting up a workshop. But now that he's put down roots in Windham, New Hampshire, he's able at last to indulge his passion for building things. He recently built bunk beds for his grandsons' bedroom, designing the beds to fit into a small bedroom that has a pitched ceiling and a protruding chimney. To get the beds up a narrow stairway, Cliff built them in eight sections that could be reassembled. He used select-grade fir 2x4s and 1-in. pine boards screwed together with McFeely's coated steel square-drive wood screws. Cliff further customized the beds with a clothes tree fashioned from a sugar maple branch, bookcase headboards with built-in reading lights, and secret compartments where each boy can stash personal treasures. Finally, he personalized each bed by routing his grandsons' names on the sides.

A Very Finished Basement

Bob Pfaffinger and his family like to hang out in their basement. That's not surprising since it opens onto one of the many picturesque duck ponds in their Plymouth, Minnesota, neighborhood. Of course, it also helps that Bob turned the place into a comfortable retreat. It features a pool table, entertainment center, bar, bathroom, and a poker room. The basement was unfinished when he bought the house six years ago. He installed tongue-and-groove wall paneling, an acoustic ceiling, lighting, and built the bar and the bathroom. His latest handiwork is the pair of cedar Adirondack chairs. "When it's winter in Minnesota, I like to have an indoor project to keep busy," Bob explains. Looks like he's earned a summer off.

The Never-Ending Remodeling Job

John Wandling started remodeling his Vancouver, Washington, condominium thinking he could do the work within a $10,000 budget. Three years and $25,000 later, he's still finding projects to tackle, but his most extensive creation to date is this remodeled kitchen. A master machinist by trade, John is new to woodworking. He bought a book to help him calculate basic cabinet dimensions, but he and his wife, Jenny, did the actual design themselves.

John built all the cabinets pictured here, laid the hardwood floor and installed the garden window. He made the two wooden stools with leftovers from the $2,000 worth of wood he purchased.

As often happens, the rehab turned up other things that needed fixing. John replaced aluminum wiring and galvanized

water lines with copper, and upgraded outdated recessed lighting with code-approved fixtures. The project was ambitious, considering John did much of the work with hand tools. Believe it or not, his only stationary power tool is a 40-year-old Delta Rockwell table saw, and his only portable power tool is a small router.

▼ Greenhouse Without Much Green

When Danny Rogers and his wife, Jackie, of Brunswick, Georgia, wanted a greenhouse, they were put off by the cost of the greenhouse kits. So Danny figured out a way to build one himself. The frame for his 120 square foot greenhouse is galvanized conduit, and is anchored to the ground with steel rebar. Clear polycarbonate panels, which he purchased from a home center, make up the roof and walls. Each panel is attached to the frame with sheet metal screws fitted with rubber O-rings to make them weathertight. He got the O-rings by stripping them off roofing nails. He also installed underground water and power lines, as well as a cooling fan and a sprinkler system. Danny's proud of his project, particularly because he spent less than $1,000 to build it.

Recycled Cedar Tree ▶

A year and a half ago, this chest of drawers was a Christmas tree growing in the front yard of Frank Morgan's sister's house in Graysville, Tennessee. The 45-year-old red cedar had grown too large and had to be removed, but Frank saw an opportunity in the loss. He saved the wood and had it milled into 1-in. boards at the local sawmill. After letting it dry for a year, he built this chest. There's no stain on this beauty—the red is the cedar's natural color.

A construction equipment operator by trade, Frank worked on the chest in his spare time. He designed the piece himself, even fashioning the drawer pulls from cedar scraps. A great niece has already laid claim to this chest as a place to store her clothes, but Frank's not concerned. He says there's enough lumber left over to make another chest of drawers just like this one.

Large Table, Short Stock

How do you build a large table from short stock? "All it takes is a good design," explains Ted Neff of St. Charles, Illinois. Ted designed this table on his home computer and built it from 1-in. x 6-in. x 4-ft. redwood boards. By branching out from the center in a starburst pattern, Ted was able to make the diameter of the table double that of his shortest board. Ted's biggest challenge was cutting the tapered pieces for the octagonal table top. He cut all of the pieces on his table saw using a tapering jig. While the project took nearly all of Ted's spare time last summer, he's ready to tackle another project this spring that makes creative use of unusual building materials.

Green Thumb Handyman

Club member Bud Cole of Olney, Maryland, had never been able to find a seedling rack that really worked well for the many plants his wife, Arlene, started from seed. In need of an effective system that could be adjusted as seedlings grew, Bud designed and built this rack. Not only did he use woodworking and wiring skills, but he even used a bit of physics in the design. Here is how his rack works: Four lights are suspended from joists with ropes and pulleys, all of which lead back to an indexed adjustment system. As the plants germinate and grow, the lights can be raised easily to the perfect height. In keeping with the "green" theme, most of the project was built with recycled wood from pallets and remodeling projects.

▼ Frugal Functionality

Club member Terry Lynch of Carmel, Indiana, doesn't believe in wasting anything. He saves virtually all wood scraps and leftover paint, no matter how little, from his basement workshop projects. As you can see here, his waste-not/want-not philosophy pays off. Terry constructed this decorative room divider mostly out of scrap-box oak and a variety of old paint. He made this piece for a wedding gift, but kept a pine version for himself to serve a very functional purpose. When the leaves are off the trees, sunlight pours in through the west-facing windows in his family room. Terry positioned his divider near the windows to block the sun's glare on the television screen.

▲ New Old Phone

Member William Mann of Sedalia, Missouri, thought the touch-tone telephone in his brother's century-old Victorian home looked out of place. So when his brother became engaged, William, a mechanical designer, knew what he'd give the couple— a reproduction antique wall phone. He designed the piece in a computer-aided design (CAD) drafting class, using an antique phone as a model. Once back in his workshop, he dismantled a spare phone for its circuit board, touch pad, earpiece, and microphone. Then he transplanted the parts to the new cabinet. He turned the oak earpiece on his lathe and fabricated the voice coil housing and arm from aluminum and brass.

Nails? No

When David Neuwirth of Mukwonago, Wisconsin, takes on a project, he likes to be challenged. Even though he has built a few benches in his time, David decided to do this redwood bench differently. The only mechanical fasteners in the entire project are screws that were used in the angled braces under the seat. Everything else is doweled and glued. David says his biggest challenge was gluing up the sides to the back and seat since it all had to be assembled and clamped at once. He did manage to avoid one possible challenge: his lumberyard burned to the ground soon after he purchased the material. If he had missed a cut during construction, he would have been out of luck.

Swinging Project

Charles Beiderman likes to work with his hands. The Williamsburg, Virginia, Club member is an accomplished woodcarver (he once authored a book on the subject) and an avid do-it-yourselfer. He stays busy with challenging projects like this covered swing, which he recently built for his backyard. The design was inspired by a gazebo he saw at a friend's home.

Charles was intrigued by the prospect of building a cantilevered structure that would provide shelter from the elements without obscuring the view. With its relatively large roof and small footprint, the structure's posts would need to be rock solid. So he selected pressure-treated (ground-contact-rated) wood for the posts and set them on compacted gravel footings so the ends would not soak up moisture. Then he poured concrete around the posts to anchor them. Curved brackets between the posts and beams and the cross bucks that form the sides are both structural and decorative.

Double-Duty Furniture

Parents of young children will appreciate this coffee table/toy box, as does member Bob Frolichstein's daughter. When she asked her dad to build a coffee table that would resemble a trunk, she and her two sons got an unexpected bonus. The St. Louis, Missouri, member chamfered pieces of leftover cedar fencing and edge-glued them to form the panels. He then fabricated the corner guards out of pieces of aluminum. The rounded corners offer some peace of mind when the kids are about. To open the large toy drawer, you just pull on the (lockless) hasp. Dual casters allow the drawer to roll out easily on the carpet. They also support the weight so the case doesn't tip when the drawer is extended.

Handy Hoist

Richard Bornert was tired of carrying shingles up a ladder. So the 70-year-old Alhambra, Illinois, member combined his welding and woodworking skills to construct this shingle hoist. Richard took an old 18-ft. ladder and attached 1x1-in. steel angle irons to each side rail. He then made a hoisting dolly from 2-in. angle irons and ½-in.-thick plywood. He welded four garage door rollers to the dolly's sides, which allow it to roll up and down the angle iron track on the ladder's side rails. A geared winch with ¼-in. cable is attached to the dolly, which is then powered by a ½-in. portable drill fitted with a universal joint and socket. According to Richard, the hoist will lift three bundles of shingles to a height of 17 feet in two minutes. Richard spent two weeks and less than $100 on the project. "I never have any help, so I always need to find ways to do things myself," he explains. He's already planning his second roofing project.

Direct Hit With Avid Hunter

Although Ronald Leeman is a retired postal employee, he worked for many years before that as a carpenter. Now this Casco, Maine, Club member is back in the construction business, doing remodeling work and building furniture for friends and family members. He recently completed a gun cabinet for his son-in-law, who is an avid hunter. Ronald started with just two specifications: The piece would be made from pine, and it had to have locks to keep the weapons and ammunition away from curious kids. The cabinet is 6-foot-6. On the inside are felt-covered brackets to hold the shotguns and rifles. Two drawers at the base of the cabinet have ample room for storing ammunition. And all of the compartments have locks. As you might expect, the project was a (direct) hit with his son-in-law.

Modern Cabinet With Vintage Past

Club member Robert Bumpus takes his inspiration where he finds it. In this case, the New York City home remodeling contractor and cabinet-maker spotted a discarded yellow cedar wine barrel in a trash dumpster. Even before he got the sweet salvage back to his workshop, he started to imagine its rebirth in the form of the cabinet you see here.

Building straight case and door frames from curved stock is no small task. Robert started by developing and refining the design with a scale model of the real thing. Then he set out to prepare the wood. One thing Robert didn't count on was the endless hours needed to chip and scrape the ½-in.-thick, decades-old wine residue by hand from the inside faces of the boards. With the stock cleaned, he planed the broad surfaces of the barrel staves. Then he resawed the angled side edges and squared them on his jointer. While the case frame, door frame, legs, and top are made from the barrel staves, the hand-crafted door handles are walnut and the door panels are hardboard.

Although the project was more work than he anticipated, Robert says it was worth the extra effort to create a piece of furniture that started its life with a rich heritage.

A Real Do-It-Yourselfer

Even as a child, Club member Kristin Koch-Wahl, from Minnetonka, Minnesota, admired her grandmother's Jenny Lind-style bed. As an adult, she hoped that one day the bed would be passed on to her. When that didn't happen, she decided she'd have to make one for herself just like it. The fact that she'd never turned wood was not a deterrent. Her confidence was high because she had plenty of experience maintaining

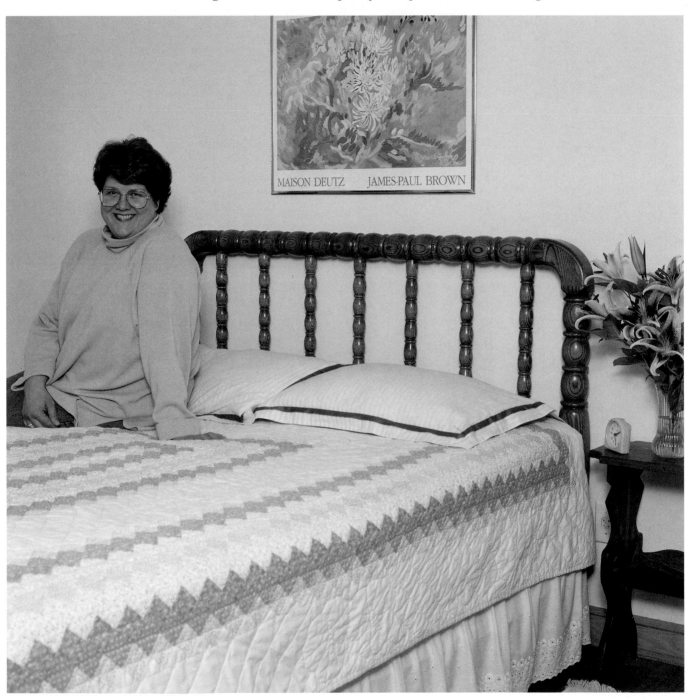

and repairing her own home. So Kristin simply enrolled in a local woodworking class and spent a winter and spring working on her project. With the help of her instructor, she worked out a design, chose a wood (oak), and learned to use a variety of tools. The majority of her shop time, however, was spent learning to use a lathe to turn pieces. Now that she's acquired some serious woodworking skills, Kristin faces an even bigger challenge finding spare time in her busy life to use them. May we suggest a clock project?

Is It a Stool or a Chair?

Although Club member Tom Darswell's passion is carving, the Sacramento, California, woodworker tried his hand at furniture making to build this unique piece for his daughter. Flip the red oak chair up and it becomes a light-duty step stool. He hand cut the mortise and tenons, and used biscuit joinery for the first time. Still, he couldn't resist decorating the piece with some of his signature carving. Note the horse's head across the backrest.

Environmentally Savvy Handyman

Most people buy electric trickle chargers to revive their vehicle
or boat batteries. Not Club member Harry Troup of Roanoke,
Indiana. Instead, he built a windmill to do the job. He placed a
battery inside the windmill's 3-ft.-tall body and hooked it up to
a 12-volt alternator he salvaged from a car's electrical system.
The blades turn a long belt, which in turn spin the alternator
and create electricity to charge the battery. Harry mounted the
windmill on a lazy Susan and added a rudder that acts like a
weathervane and always points into the wind.

Look At That Bar

Ask Joe Wayman of Elsberry, Missouri, how many of his collectibles are stashed away in his closets and he'll proudly tell you "none!" Belly up to the bar that he recently finished and you'll see why. It doubles as a display case for his family heirlooms. The design was inspired by the glass-topped tables at a well-known restaurant on Captiva Island, just off Florida's west coast. Except for plumbing the sink and cutting the glass, this Club member did all of the work himself. He finished the project in about three months by working nights and weekends. With such an interesting view, this is one bar where coasters should be optional.

◀ Maximizing Minimum Space

It's not until you look closely that you discover that Mark Vadenais' latest project—a TV cabinet for his bedroom—is actually a built-in. This seemed the best way for the North Smithfield, Rhode Island, Club member to maximize what little space he had to work with. Building a frame on only two sides and hanging the shelves on two walls made construction easier and faster.

Mark also maximized his resources for the cabinet: He used white pine remnants from the recent construction of his home. To make the cabinet an integral part of the room, he matched the cabinet's hardware to the room's.

Mark's interest (and skills) in both cabinetry and construction began when he was a youngster working under the tutelage of the late Rev. Ronaldo Gadoury, his parish priest. Today he not only does building projects around his home, he builds homes. He's been a post-and-beam contractor for nine years.

Neighborly Handyman

Club member Jeff Robertson of Middletown, Maryland, has created something of a cottage industry building entertainment centers, provided he doesn't run out of neighbors. His latest projects have been inspired by them.

Neighbor number one needed a corner cabinet to hold a TV, VCR, and Nintendo system. Since the cabinet had to fit in a restricted space, Jeff used his computer to determine the smallest interior dimensions that would still allow a TV to fit inside with adequate ventilation. He built the cabinet out of pine, concealing the TV behind raised panel doors, and the Nintendo and VCR behind flip-down drawer fronts. Neighbor number two requested a similar cabinet to be built out of birch. Assembly had been difficult with the first unit, so Jeff built a stand to hold the three sections of the second cabinet upright during assembly and gluing. Because the angles of the cabinet face made it difficult to assemble the front pieces, Jeff designed special jigs to aid in clamping glued-up pieces. After applying a natural finish, the second project was complete. Now we're wondering, Jeff, which neighbor will be the lucky recipient of your next cabinetry efforts?

You Could Live Here

The panoramic view of the Cuyahoga River valley inspired member John Jones of Akron, Ohio, to build a four-season gazebo complete with all the comforts of home. The octagonal structure has eight skylights, four casement windows, and three picture windows, and it is warmed by a natural gas space heater that's vented through a wall. John can enjoy a soft drink from the refrigerator, watch his 25-in. color TV, and communicate with the outside world via telephone or intercom.

Made primarily from cedar and cedar shakes, the interior walls are 8 feet high and reach a peak of 17½ feet. The octagon-shaped room has a 12-ft. diameter.

As beautiful as the site is, it gave John some major construction challenges. For one thing, the gazebo rests on a deck which had to be built into the side of a hill. Seven 4x6 treated posts rest on 12-in.-diameter pilings. Each footing was hand-dug 4 feet into the ground and reinforced with four 36-in. rebars. To be sure his design was structurally sound, John had an architect look over his plans before he began construction.

His next challenge was the actual gazebo construction. Six of the eight exterior walls had to be built while standing on a fully extended 32-ft. ladder. And the 1x8 cedar skylight frames required compound-miter cuts with angled dadoes.

It took John nine months and about $10,000 to single-handedly complete the project. John says he'd do it all again, "but I'd make the deck even larger!"

Atop His Shop

The Sky's the limit for devoted woodworker Tom Meade of Minnetonka, Minnesota. His latest project: a cupola perched neatly atop his garage workshop. Complete with louvers and a weathervane, projects like this are regular sustenence for Tom. "I subscribe to every woodworking magazine produced," he boasts. He refurbishes tools, too.

Tom spent several hours and $50 building and finishing the cupola in his workshop. To speed up the project, he used ready-made fixed louvers. Then he strapped a rope around the completed structure and hoisted it to the roof. Tom secured the cupola by screwing through the sides into a couple of 2x4 cleats he first attached to the roof.

What was his favorite part of the project? "Everything," he says. "I got to practice all my skills—design, layout, building, painting, and shingling."

Now with the cupola in place, there's just one problem: "My wife says the weathervane doesn't point north. I think she's right!"

His Bi-Level Best ▶

Inspried by the land surrounding his home in Puyallup, Washington, Retired Col. James Sands Jr. designed and built a deck of beauty, precision, and efficiency. The two-level cedar and treated-lumber structure nestles snugly between the rolling terrain and the back of his house. James designed built-in benches and flower boxes to serve double-duty as deck railings. To preserve this $3,950 work of

art (and three weeks of sweat!), he treated the entire deck with BEHR linseed oil-based stain/sealant, applied with a Wagner Power Painter. And the flowers? James credits his "wife's green thumb" for that finishing touch.

The Best Laid Plans ▶

Eagan, Minnesota, member Dave Moench took his own advice when he built his fireplace hearth and mantel: "One hour of planning is worth 10 hours of work and $100 in material." When Dave's home was under construction, he wasn't ready to install the fireplace, but he planned for one just the same and had his builder install the chimney and required block. Then, when he was ready to install the fireplace, he talked to dealers and designed the installation on paper first. His design for the granite hearth and wood mantel was inspired after many visits to showrooms and discussions with code officials. Even after the installation was underway, planning took precedence as he measured dimensions carefully before ordering the stone for the hearth and the wood for the mantel.

Dave's planning and DIY efforts saved him a considerable amount of money. He spent $3,100 and estimates a builder would have charged $4,800. While he's pleased with his project, he offers another bit of sage advice for fellow members and DIYers to remember: "Don't be afraid to hire professionals to tackle parts you are not capable of doing."

Garden Elegance ▶

As a construction supervisor, Vincent Falini actually gets little opportunity to work with his hands on the job. Once he gets home, the Dunedin, Florida, member can't wait to dig into a project. Vincent's latest effort is this fir garden bench. It's finished with primer and two coats of high-gloss enamel.

A Crowning Achievement

Bob Kochis of Trumbull, Connecticut, makes teeth (crowns, actually) for a living, and no two are exactly alike. This proved to be excellent training for the fieldstone patio he built alongside his new sunroom.

Bob found it very difficult to cut the heavily stratified rock with a hammer and a chisel. So he was forced to assemble this incredible mosaic by hunting for the best stone to fill each gap.

He started by edging the free-form shape with cobblestone, then he concentrated on the middle. As in his one-person business, Bob knew how to make every move count. Rather than trial fit a number of stones until he discovered the one that worked best, he sketched the next space on a pad and took his drawing to the rock pile to locate the perfect piece to fill it.

If you are considering a fieldstone project, Bob offers the following advice: "Be sure you look at the stone in the supply yard. Don't rely on the samples in the showroom because there can be quite a difference from lot to lot. I picked the two pallets I like best and had the guy tag them right away."

Bob completed the project in four days. That included excavating the site about 8 inches, compacting the crushed rock base, fitting the stones and setting them with dry ready-mix mortar and a fine mist from his garden hose.

"Everybody told me there was no way I could finish it in four days, but I figure I can do anything in four days," he recalled. On day five, it was back to making teeth. Using the patio had to wait.

◀ One More Time

The clocks designed and built by Harry Morehead of Parkersburg, West Virginia, give new meaning to the phrase "scrap wood." Harry's clock designs are inspired by the sizes of the wood he uses: cedar and walnut firewood, redwood from silos, and oak scraps from lumberyards.

Harry's efficiencies go beyond his use of materials. In producing his clocks, he uses a band saw to cut parts for two to four clocks at one time. He adds ready-made inserts for the clock mechanism and finishes the clocks with Formby's high-gloss polyurethane.

Tabletop Trickery ▶

Member Kevin Wade of Algoma, Wisconsin, wanted to create an end table of a different stripe when he designed and built the one pictured here. To produce the three-dimensional effect, he glued walnut, mahogany, and birch boards together; then he miter-cut and reglued them. He bordered the pattern with solid strips of mahogany and walnut, and even inlaid a brass band around the oak frame.

Not Your Grandfather's Clock

Member Bob Meyer of Elgin, Minnesota, raises seed corn for a living and builds clocks for a hobby. This "mega clock" stands eight feet tall and weighs nearly 200 pounds. It's powered by a low-speed ceiling fan motor. The large gears are made of ¾-in. plywood and the pinion gears that drive them are steel. The clock's vertical supports are ¾-in. steel electrical conduit covered with polished aluminum bathroom tubing. Although it's clearly built for looks, the clock keeps time accurately. Bob claims it loses only one second every three months, but who's counting?

Niece Pleaser

Club member Robert Hales from Hamburg, Arkansas, received three hugs—one for each mirror—from his niece when he presented her with this red oak dressing table last year. While he currently works as a maintenance supervisor for a public school, Robert had worked as a carpenter. Over the years, he has tackled many projects including building his own home, but he'd never worked with red oak or turned wood on a lathe before this project.

Same Old House, New Kitchen

It was a dark and crowded kitchen that convinced Oliver (Bud) Campbell and his wife, LeAnn, of Lamar, Missouri, to do a complete makeover. To get ideas for the design and construction of the oak cabinets, Bud made lots of trips to home centers. Then, over the course of a year, he built the cabinets in his backyard workshop out of solid wood and veneered plywood. Once he completed the 11 units, he removed the old cabinets and installed the new ones. The new kitchen boasts an efficient pantry with slide-out shelves, a lazy Susan corner cabinet, and an appliance garage with a tambour door that Bud made from scratch. The cabinet doors were hung with European-style hidden hinges that Bud says were a challenge to install but give the kitchen a clean look.

Learning How To Use Space

Robert Jordan needed a multipurpose area for home-schooling his daughter, using his computer equipment, and for storing books. His solution was to design and build a home office, utilizing the space-and his budget-efficiently. By using both new and salvaged material, this Tuleta, Texas, member was able to keep the cost of the project under $250. Robert built the cases out of birch, and glued, nailed, and screwed them together. He used plastic laminate over plywood to make the top and added red oak trim on the edges. To help keep the work top clutter-free, he cut access holes for computer wires and a slot through which printer paper is fed. Although he owns quite a few tools, Robert is particularly fond of his air nailer because it saved a lot of wear and tear on his elbow while completing the project.

Congratulatory Buffet

Ronald Pitt, a Club member from Southington, Connecticut, has been busy recently pursuing his favorite hobby— and making wedding gifts for his kids. This buffet, which he built for his son and daughter-in-law, is the second one he's made. He built it out of pine using mostly traditional woodworking joinery, including dado, rabbet, and mortise-and-tenon joints. He used plate-joining biscuits where they worked to his advantage. The cabinet is made in two sections so it can be moved easily. The top section has lights to illuminate items on display. Ronald says the most difficult parts of the project were making the arched door rails, and building a strong base. Ronald designed the doors so that the glass can be replaced easily if broken. Perhaps he's already looking ahead to grandchildren!

Personalized Furniture

A picture in a magazine inspired member Ralph Marshall of Elkins, New Hampshire, to build this oak entertainment center. However, he substantially changed the original design so he could call it his own. Instead of having two doors like the original, Ralph made his with four doors to hide electronic gear not being used. And he added decorative details such as the dentil molding around the top. He found installing the pocket doors to be the most demanding task because it required him to build the cabinet using double-wall construction. Except for the drawer sides, which are dovetailed, the unit was assembled using dadoes, grooves, and biscuits. Ralph is especially proud of this project because he's new to woodworking and he's learned techniques primarily from reading magazines.

Learn As You Go

Anticipating the need for extra storage space in her new home, Carole Johanson of Woodbury, Tennessee, had the builder frame the attic knee walls so she could build and install her own custom bookshelves. In preparation, Carole honed her skills at Shaker Village workshops in New Hampshire, and at woodworking courses she took at local technical schools. She used medium density fiberboard (MDF) for the bookshelves. Although she is pleased with the results, Carole says she will use another material for her next project. She didn't like the fine dust created by MDF. It was particularly annoying because she built the project during a hot Tennessee summer, without air conditioning.

◄ Keep On Truckin'

For George Eckhart of Kenosha, Wisconsin, work and play go hand in hand. With 33 years' experience building fire trucks and another 10 as a welder/fabricator, George is able to use real-world know-how to build scale model trucks. George constructs his trucks entirely from scratch using various bits of wood, metal, and rubber. He painstakingly built a 63-in.-long 1986 Mack tractor-trailer, and a 27½-in.-long 1988 International Harvester dump truck, which together took five years of his spare time to complete.

A skilled craftsman (he proudly boasts that he's got one of the best-equipped private workshops in his area), George has built more than 50 clocks, including grandfathers, both for his home and for others. Now that he's retired, George is using his free time to complete work on another truck, a 22-in.-long 1938 GMC pickup. He's also busy making two dozen pen and pencil sets, all from a variety of exotic woods.

Secret Treasure

Club member Craig Nelson of St. Anthony, Idaho, a custom woodworker for nine years, knows how to deliver when a special gift is called for. Recently, Craig built a solid cherry jewelry box for his wife. His future sister-in-law then requested a similar one as a wedding gift. Each box measures about 19 inches tall, 9 inches wide, and 6 inches deep and features raised panel doors, a hidden compartment in the top and two felt-lined drawers. Although Craig typically works on larger pieces such as gun cabinets, entertainment centers, and bedroom sets, he seems to be just as comfortable with his smaller projects.

A Matter of Time

Ask member Rhett Allen of McPherson, Kansas, what tool is best for constructing one of his intricate fretwork clocks, and he'll quickly reply, "Good eyes!" He speaks from experience; one dome clock he built took four weeks just to cut the pieces.

Rhett built the cathedral clock shown here using a purchased pattern. It measures 32 inches high, 18 inches wide, and 5 inches deep. The wood for the clock came from a cedar tree he had removed from his yard to make way for remodeling project some years ago.

A retired military man, Rhett spends his time tinkering and building various times such as picture frames, plaques, and clocks. Although he doesn't believe in selling the fruits of his labor, he has built for friends, neighbors, and relatives. With more time now for hobbies, Rhett is ready, willing and able to learn some new tricks—like power carving, which he took up just last year. No doubt, we'll be seeing more of his work.

reference

Dimensional Stability of Various Hardwoods
Natural Resistance to Shrinking and Swelling

Greater Resistance		Lower Resistance	
Group I	*Group II*	*Group III*	*Group IV*
Black/brown ash	Red alder	Beech	Cottonwood
White ash	Aspen	Red gum	Black gum
Butternut	Basswood	Magnolia	Sap gum
Cherry	Birch	Red oak	Sycamore
Chestnut	Buckeye	Tupelo	
Walnut	Rock elm		
Willow	Soft elm		
Hackberry			
Hard maple			
Oregon maple			
Soft maple			
White oak			
Poplar			

Pilot Hole/Shank Clearance Hole Boring Recommendations

	Bit or Drill Sizes						
	For shank- clearance holes		For pilot holes				
			Hardwoods		Softwoods		
	Twist bit	Drill gauge	Twist bit	Drill gauge no.	Twist bit	Drill gauge no.	Auger bit no.
Screw no.	Nearest size in fractions of an inch	to be used for maximum holding power	Nearest size in fractions of an inch	to be used for maximum holding power	Nearest size in fractions of an inch	to be used for maximum holding power	to counter-bore for sinking head {by 16ths}
0	$1/16$	52	$1/32$	70	$1/64$	75	
1	$5/64$	47	$1/32$	66	$1/32$	71	
2	$3/32$	42	$3/64$	56	$1/32$	65	3
3	$7/64$	37	$1/16$	54	$3/64$	58	4
4	$7/64$	32	$1/16$	52	$3/64$	55	4
5	$1/8$	30	$5/64$	49	$1/16$	53	4
6	$9/64$	27	$5/64$	47	$1/16$	52	5
7	$5/32$	22	$3/32$	44	$1/16$	51	5
8	$11/64$	18	$3/32$	40	$5/64$	48	6
9	$3/16$	14	$7/64$	37	$5/64$	45	6
10	$3/16$	10	$7/64$	33	$3/32$	43	6
11	$13/64$	4	$1/8$	31	$3/32$	40	7
12	$7/32$	2	$1/8$	30	$7/64$	38	7
14	$1/4$	D	$9/64$	25	$7/64$	32	8
16	$17/64$	I	$5/32$	18	$9/64$	29	9
18	$19/64$	N	$3/16$	13	$9/64$	26	10
20	$21/64$	P	$13/64$	4	$11/64$	19	11
24	$3/8$	V	$7/32$	1	$3/16$	15	12

Standard Sizes of Yard Lumber

Type of Lumber	Nominal size (in inches)		Actual size (in inches)	
	Thickness	*Width*	*Thickness*	*Width*
Dimension	2	4	1½	3½
	2	6	1½	5½
	2	8	1½	7¼
	2	10	1½	9¼
	2	12	1½	11¼
Timbers	4	6	3½	5½
	4	8	3½	7¼
	4	10	3½	9¼
	6	6	5½	5½
	6	8	5½	7¼
	6	10	5½	9¼
	8	8	7¼	7¼
	8	10	7¼	9¼
Common boards	1	4	¾	3½
	1	6	¾	5½
	1	8	¾	7¼
	1	10	¾	9¼
	1	12	¾	11¼

Characteristics of Many Common Woods

Species	Comparative Weights	Color	Handtool Working	Nailability	Relative Density	General Strength	Resistance to Decay	Wood Finishing	Cost
Hardwoods									
Apitong	Heavy	Reddish Brown	Hard	Poor	Medium	Good	High	Poor	Medium High
Ash, Brown	Medium	Light Brown	Medium	Medium	Hard	Medium	Low	Medium	Medium
Ash, Tough White	Heavy	Off-white	Hard	Poor	Hard	Good	Low	Medium	Medium
Ash, Soft White	Medium	Off-white	Medium	Medium	Medium	Low	Low	Medium	Medium Low
Avodire	Medium	Golden Blond	Medium	Medium	Medium	Low	Low	Medium	High
Balsawood	Light	Cream White	Easy	Good	Soft	Low	Low	Poor	Medium
Basswood White	Light	Cream	Easy	Good	Soft	Low	Low	Medium	Medium
Beech	Heavy	Light Brown	Hard	Poor	Hard	Good	Low	Easy	Medium
Birch	Heavy	Light Brown	Hard	Poor	Hard	Good	Low	Easy	High
Butternut	Light	Light Brown	Easy	Good	Soft	Low	Medium	Medium	Medium
Cherry, Black	Medium	Reddish Medium Brown	Hard	Poor	Hard	Good	Medium	Easy	High

Species	Comparative Weights	Color	Handtool Working	Nailability	Relative Density	General Strength	Resistance to Decay	Wood Finishing	Cost
Chestnut Brown	Light	Light	Medium	Medium	Medium	Medium	High	Poor	Medium
Cottonwood	Light	Grayish White	Medium	Good	Soft	Low	Low	Poor	Low
Elm, Soft, Northern	Medium	Cream Tan	Hard	Good	Medium	Medium	Medium	Medium	Medium Low
Gum, Red	Medium	Reddish Brown	Medium	Medium	Medium	Medium	Medium	Medium	Medium High
Hickory, True	Heavy	Reddish Tan	Hard	Poor	Hard	Good	Low	Medium	Low
Holly	Medium	White to Gray	Medium	Medium	Hard	Medium	Low	Easy	Medium
Limba	Medium	Pale Golden	Medium	Good	Medium	Medium	Low	Medium	High
Magnolia	Medium	Yellowish Brown	Medium	Medium	Medium	Medium	Low	Easy	Medium
Mahogany, Honduras	Medium	Golden Brown	Easy	Good	Medium	Medium	High	Medium	High
Mahogany, Philippine	Medium	Medium Red	Easy	Good	Medium	Medium	High	Medium	Medium High
Maple, Hard	Heavy	Reddish Cream	Hard	Poor	Hard	Good	Low	Easy	Medium High
Maple, Soft	Medium	Reddish Brown	Hard	Poor	Hard	Good	Low	Easy	Medium Low
Oak, Red (avg.)	Heavy	Flesh	Hard Brown	Medium	Hard	Good	Low	Medium	Medium

Characteristics of Many Common Woods (continued)

Species	Comparative Weights	Color	Handtool Working	Nailability	Relative Density	General Strength	Resistance to Decay	Wood Finishing	Cost
Oak, White (avg.)	Heavy Grayish	Brown	Hard	Medium	Hard	Good	High	Medium	Medium High
Poplar, Yellow	Medium	Light to Dark Yellow	Easy	Good	Soft	Low	Low	Easy	Medium
Primavera	Medium	Straw Tan	Medium	Medium	Medium	Medium	Medium	Medium	High
Sycamore	Medium	Flesh Brown	Hard	Good	Medium	Medium	Low	Easy	Medium Low
Walnut, Black	Heavy	Brown Dark	Medium	Medium	Hard	Good	High	Medium	High
Willow, Black	Light	Medium Brown	Easy	Good	Soft	Low	Low	Medium	LowMedium
Softwoods									
Cedar, Tennessee Red	Medium	Red	Medium	Poor	Medium	Medium	High	Easy	Medium
Cypress	Medium	Yellow to Reddish	Medium	Good	Soft	Medium	High	Poor	Medium High
Fir, Douglas	Medium	Orange Brown	Medium	Poor	Soft	Medium	Medium	Poor	Medium
Fir, White	Light	Nearly White	Medium	Poor	Soft	Low	Low	Poor	Low
Pine, Yellow Longleaf	Medium	Orange to Reddish Brown	Hard	Poor	Medium	Good	Medium	Medium	Medium High

Member Tips and Projects

Species	Comparative Weights	Color	Handtool Working	Nailability	Relative Density	General Strength	Resistance to Decay	Wood Finishing	Cost
Pine, Eastern White	Light	Cream to Reddish Brown	Easy	Good	Soft	Low	Medium	Medium	Medium High
Pine, Ponderosa	Light	Orange to Reddish Brown	Easy	Good	Soft	Low	Low	Medium	Medium
Pine, Sugar	Light	Creamy Brown	Easy	Good	Soft	Low	Medium	Poor	Medium High
Redwood	Light	Deep Reddish Brown	Easy	Good	Soft	Medium	High	Poor	Medium
Spruces (avg.)	Light	Nearly White	Medium	Medium	Soft	Low	Low	Medium	Medium

Slotted Screw Tool Selector

Screw Size	Blade Size	Screw Size	Blade Size
0	$3/32$"	9	$5/16$"
1	$3/32$"	10	$5/16$"
2	$1/8$"	12	$3/8$"
3	$5/32$"	14	$3/8$"
4	$3/16$"	16	$7/16$"
5	$3/16$"	18	$7/16$"
6	$1/4$"	20	$1/2$"
7	$1/4$"	24	$1/2$"
8	$5/16$"		

Too narrow   *Too thin*   *Too wide*   *Correct*

Drill Sizes For Slotted Wood Screws

Screw Size	Body Hole Size		Lead Hole Size				Bit Size In 16ths For Counterbore
			Hardwoods		Softwoods		
	Nearest Fractional Size Drill	Accurate Drill Size No./Lettersize	Nearest Fractional SizeDrill	Nearest Accurate Drill Size	Fractional Size Drill	Accurate Drill Size	
0	1/16	52	1/32	70			
1	5/64	47	1/32	66	1/32	71	
2	3/32	42	3/64	56	1/32	65	3
3	7/64	37	1/16	54	3/64	58	4
4	7/64	32	1/16	52	3/64	55	4
5	1/8	30	5/64	49	1/16	53	4
6	9/64	27	5/64	47	1/16	52	5
7	5/32	22	3/32	44	1/16	51	5
8	11/64	18	3/32	40	5/64	48	6
9	3/16	14	7/64	37	5/64	45	6
10	3/16	10	7/64	33	3/32	43	6
11	13/64	4	1/8	31	3/32	40	7
12	7/32	2	1/8	30	7/64	38	8
14	1/4	D	9/64	25	7/64	32	8
16	17/64	I	5/32	18	9/64	29	9
18	19/64	N	3/16	13	9/64	26	10
20	21/64	P	13/64	4	11/64	19	11
24	3/8	V	7/32	1	3/16	15	12

Lead holes are seldom used for Nos. 0 and 1 gauge screws.
In softwood, lead holes are unnecessary for gauges less than No. 6.

Nails
Common Nails—Actual Size

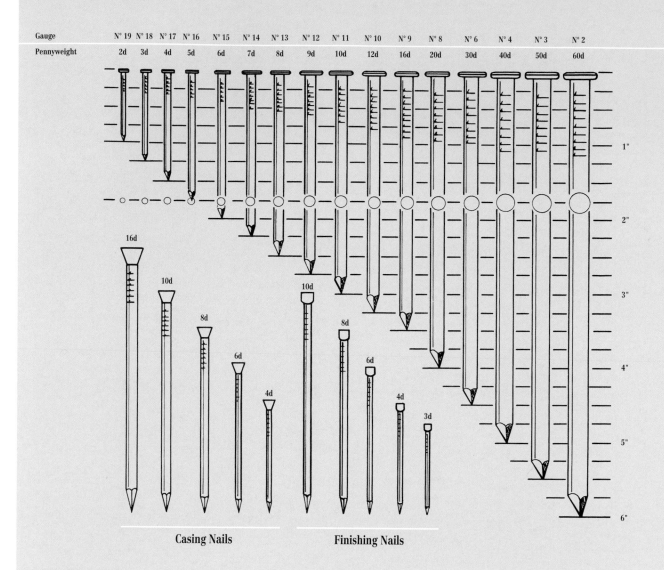

Gauge	N° 19	N° 18	N° 17	N° 16	N° 15	N° 14	N° 13	N° 12	N° 11	N° 10	N° 9	N° 8	N° 6	N° 4	N° 3	N° 2
Pennyweight	2d	3d	4d	5d	6d	7d	8d	9d	10d	12d	16d	20d	30d	40d	50d	60d

Casing Nails   Finishing Nails

Materials & Finishes

Copper: rustproof

Brass: rustproof

Bronze: rustproof

Steel: not rust resistant

Stainless Steel: rustproof, corrosion-resistant

Electro-zinc plated steel: interior

Galvanized: some rust resistance

Hot-dipped galvanized: rust resistant

Cement-coated: short term holding power (box & crate construction)

Blued, heat-treated: temporary rust resistance (indoors)

Bright: not corrosion-resistant

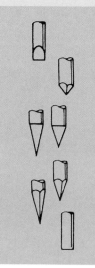

Nail Points

Chisel (Wedge) Point Nails are used with the point oriented cross-grain. The nail thus cuts its way into the wood and penetrates well without causing splits. Use with dense woods.

Blunt Diamond Nails punch their way into the wood; do not cause splitting and have better holding power than pointier nails. Hard woods, hardwood.

Long Needle & Round Or Short Needle Use with medium & soft woods and composition boards in which they spread the fibres instead of splitting them.

Long Diamond Or Regular Diamond General commercial use. To prevent splitting, blunt the point before using.

Square End Nails reduces splitting but has reduced withdrawal resistance due to destruction of fibres.

Chart of Compound Angles for Band Saw & Table Saw

Tilt Of Work	Equivalent Taper/Inch	Four-sided Butt		Four-sided Mitre		Six-sided Mitre		Eight-sided Mitre	
		Bevel Degress	*Mitre Degrees*	*Bevel Degress*	*Mitre Degrees*	*Bevel Degress*	*Mitre Degrees*	*Bevel Degress*	*Mitre Degrees*
5°	0.087	½	85	44¾	85	29¾	87½	22¼	88
10°	0.176	1½	80¼	44¼	80¼	29½	84½	22	86
15°	0.268	3¾	75½	43¼	75½	29	81¾	21½	84
20°	0.364	6¼	71¼	41¾	71¼	28¼	79	21	82
25°	0.466	10	67	40	67	27¼	76½	20¼	80
30°	0.577	14½	63½	37¾	63½	26	74	19½	78¼
35°	0.700	19½	60¼	35½	60¼	24½	71¾	18¼	76¾
40°	0.839	24½	57¼	32½	57¼	22¾	69¾	17	75
45°	1.000	30	54¾	30	54¾	21	67¾	15¾	73¾
50°	1.19	36	52½	27	52½	19	66¼	14½	72½
55°	1.43	42	50¾	24	50¾	16¾	64¾	12½	71¼
60°	1.73	48	49	21	49	14½	63½	11	70¼

Chart of Compound Angles for Radial Saw

Tilt Of Work	Equivalent Taper/Inch	Four-sided Butt		Four-sided Mitre		Six-sided Mitre		Eight-sided Mitre	
		Bevel Degress	Mitre Degrees	Bevel Degress	Mitre Degrees	Bevel Degress	Mitre Degrees	Bevel Degress	Mitre Degrees
5°	0.087	½	5	44¾	5	29¾	2½	22¼	2
10°	0.176	1½	9¾	44¼	9¾	29½	5½	22	4
15°	0.268	3¾	14½	43¼	14½	29	8¼	21½	6
20°	0.364	6¼	18¾	41¾	18¾	28¼	11	21	8
25°	0.466	10	23	40	23	27¼	13½	20¼	10
30°	0.577	14½	26½	37¾	26½	26	16	19½	11¾
35°	0.700	19½	29¾	35½	29¾	24½	18¼	18¼	13¼
40°	0.839	24½	32¾	32½	32¾	22¾	20¼	17	15
45°	1.000	30	35¼	30	35¼	21	22¼	15¾	16¼
50°	1.19	36	37½	27	37½	19	23¾	14½	17½
55°	1.43	42	39¼	24	39¼	16¾	25¼	12½	18¾
60°	1.73	48	41	21	41	14½	26½	11	19¾

Drill Speeds in R.P.M.
For Various Materials

Diameter of Drill	Soft Metals 300 F.P.M.	Plastics and Hard Rubber 200 F.P.M.	Anneaded Cast Iron 140 F.P.M.	Mild Steel 100 F.P.M.	Malleable Iron 90 F.P.M.	Hard Cast Iron 80 F.P.M.	Tool or Hard Steel 60 F.P.M.	Alloy Steel Cast Steel 40 F.P.M.
1/16 (No. 53 to 80)	18320	12217	8554	6111	5500	4889	3667	2445
3/32 (No. 42 to 52)	12212	8142	5702	4071	3666	3258	2442	1649
1/8 (No. 31 to 41)	9160	6112	4278	3056	2750	2445	1833	1222
5/32 (No. 23 to 30)	7328	4888	3420	2444	2198	1954	1465	977
3/16 (No. 13 to 22)	6106	4075	2852	2037	1833	1630	1222	815
7/32 (No. 1 to 12)	5234	3490	2444	1745	1575	1396	1047	698
1/4 (A to E)	4575	3055	2139	1527	1375	1222	917	611
9/32 (G to K)	4071	2712	1900	1356	1222	1084	814	542
5/16 (L, M, N)	3660	2445	1711	1222	1100	978	733	489
11/32 (O to R)	3330	2220	1554	1110	1000	888	666	444
3/8 (S, T, U)	3050	2037	1426	1018	917	815	611	407
13/32 (V to Z)	2818	1878	1316	939	846	752	563	376
7/16	2614	1746	1222	873	786	698	524	349
15/32	2442	1628	1140	814	732	652	488	326
1/2	2287	1528	1070	764	688	611	458	306
9/16	2035	1357	950	678	611	543	407	271
5/8	1830	1222	856	611	550	489	367	244
11/16	1665	1110	777	555	500	444	333	222
3/4	1525	1018	713	509	458	407	306	204

Figures are for High-Speed Twist Drills.
The speed of Carbon Twist Drills should be reduced one-half.
Use drill speed nearest to figure given.

Suggested Spindle Speeds In Rpm For Twist Drills

Hole Size in Inches	Drilling Speeds*						
	Softwoods	Hardwoods	Plastics	Aluminum	Brass	Cast Iron	Mild Steel
1/16"	4700	4700	4700	4700	4700	4700	2400
1/8"	4700	4700	4700	4700	4700	2400	1250
3/16"	4700	2400	2400	4700	2400	2400	1250
1/4"	2400	2400	2400	4700	2400	1250	700
5/16"	2400	1250	1250	2400	1250	1250	700
3/8"	2400	1250	1250	2400	1250	700	700
7/16"	2400	1250	1250	1250	1250	700	
1/2"	1250	1250	1250	1250	700	700	
5/8"	1250	700	700	700			
3/4"	1250	700	700	700			
7/8"	1250	700					
1"	700	700					
1 1/4"	700	700					
1 1/2"	700	700					
2"	700	700					

*For intermediate sizes, use speed suggested for next larger hole.
Use slower speeds for deep holes or if drill bit burns or melts material.

American How-To index

If you need information that is not included in this book, chances are that *American How-To* magazine has run an article on it. To help you, we've included an index to every article the magazine has ever run. To order back issues, write to: Handyman Club Back Issues, P.O. Box 3410, Minnetonka, MN 55343. Not all issues are available.

Each entry is followed by a code identifying the issue and the page on which the topic can be found. For example: JF93-30 refers to the January/February 1993 issue, page 30. MA refers to March/April; MJ, May/June; JA, July/August; SO, September/October; ND, November/December.

polish (ND94-64)
polisher (MJ94-64)
pressure washer (JF96-62)
propane heater (JA96-68)
protective mat (JF96-65)
pruner (MJ96-70)
radial arm saw (MA96-80)
ramps (ND93-67)
reciprocating saw (MJ95-67)
router (ND94-63)
router pad (JF94-63)
ruler, adhesive-backed (MA96-84)
sanding belts (JF96-63)
sandpaper (JA94-59)
saw blade (SO94-64) (MJ95-66)
sawhorse (JF95-62) (MJ96-72) (SO96-70)
scissors (ND93-67)
screen (MA95-60)
screwdrivers (MA95-62) (MJ96-72)
scroll saw (JA95-66)
sharpener (MA94-65) (MJ94-65)
shelf, sliding (MA96-82)
shop vac (JF95-62) (MJ95-67)
snow scoop (ND96-71)
socket (JA95-67)
socket set (JA95-67)
software,
    home projects (JF96-63)
    home repair (JA96-68)
spill absorbant (SO96-70)
spindle sander (JA95-67)
    attachment (MA96-80)
spray lube (JA96-69)
square-drive screws (JF96-64)
stain (SO95-69)
    exterior (MA96-84)
    spray-on (SO96-68)
stripper (ND95-66)
string trimmer (MJ96-70)
    cordless (MA96-80)
support belt (MA94-64)
surface protector, liquid (ND96-74)
table saw (SO95-69)
table saw accessory (JA95-69)
table saw blades (JA96-67)
tape measure (JA94-60) (JF95-63)
tie-down, vehicle (ND96-73)
toilet fill valve (JF96-65)
toilet flapper (ND96-73)
tool grips (JA96-69)
toolbox (ND93-67) (JF95-64)
tote (JF94-62)
tray (JF94-62)
tweezers (MA94-65)
utility box (JA96-67)
utility cart, folding (ND96-70)
utility knife (MJ96-73)
vinyl repair (ND94-64)
vise pads (magnetic) (SO94-63)
wall/crack repair (MA95-62)
water filter (ND95-66)
weed killer, liquid (MA96-86)
wet/dry vac (JF96-63) (ND96-70)
window lock (ND94-64)

wood cleaner/sealer (ND96-73)
wood fix (ND94-64)
work light, flexible (MA96-82)
Metal snips, technique (JA94-56)
Microwave oven, installation (MJ95-46)
Modern Methods,
    basement, insulation (ND95-28)
    concrete, repair (ND94-48)
    fishing wires (MA94-22)
    floor refinishing (SO95-16)
    hot water system (MA96-32)
    keyed basement entry (JA94-12)
    patterned concrete (MJ95-50)
    removing texture (MJ94-48)
    space-saving drain (JF95-30)
    spray painting (JF94-22)
    The Nailer, drywall backer (MJ96-10)
    tiling bases (ND93-55)
    trusses, laminated wood (ND96-26)
    tubular skylight (MA95-18)
    wallpaper paneling (JF96-24)
    window film (JA95-20)
Molding,
    caulking (JA95-75)
    cornice, installing (ND95-30)
    synthetic, installing (SO94-36)
Mouse trap, review (MA96-54)
Multitesters, technique (ND96-21)

O

Outside,
    remote utilities, installation (MJ96-30)
    roof, cleaning (JA96-22)
    trees, moving (SO96-14)

P

Paint,
    ceiling fan blades, protecting (MA95-74)
    choosing (MA94-28)
    color schemes (JA96-52)
    drapes, protecting (MA95-72)
    laminate, painting (MA95-64)
    lead, removal (JA94-42)
    storing (ND93-68)
    paint splatters, removing (SO94-68)
    peeling, repair (ND96-64)
    power painter, cleaning (SO95-74)
    review (MJ95-32)
    sealant, non-toxic (ND94-60)
    spackle, priming (SO95-75)
    spraying, HVLP (JF94-22)
    technique (MA95-44)
        children (MJ94-10)
    texture, removing (MJ94-48)
    wall stripes, removing (JA94-62)
Paint brush,
    cleaning brushes (MA94-62)
    review (ND95-44)
Paneling, warped, replacing (JF96-67)
Patents, obtaining (ND96-32)
Patio, awnings (JA95-44)
Pests, controlling (SO95-60)
Piers, concrete, installing (JA96-30)
Planter/trellis, plans (MA94-14)

index